MEMORIES

——— OF AN ———

AFRICAN SUN

MARY ANN SIMKINS

TABLE OF CONTENTS

ACKNOWLEDGEMENT

A person is considered blessed if they are fortunate enough to have even one or two good friends. I have been blessed beyond what anyone could ever earn or deserve by so many vibrant, intriguing friends who gather around me like angels. You know who you are… my own dear people. You continue to make life interesting and full, and it was you who urged me to write about Africa.

Thank you to my family who are a source of continual goodness and light, and who have been so meaningfully supportive in ways that have simply made all the difference.

Beloved Megan, Keri, and Eugene—there are no words anywhere that could express how wonderful you are.

Live in the Light always.

DEDICATION

for my parents,
Cyril Simkins and Mary Shanks Simkins

Thank you for Africa

"…a light for revelation to the Gentiles…"
the words of Simeon, filled with the Holy Spirit,
as he held Jesus in his arms

AUTHOR'S NOTE

Although Zimbabwe was called Southern Rhodesia, and then just Rhodesia, during the time that I lived there, I have chosen to refer to it whenever possible by its current name of Zimbabwe, given when the nation gained its independence.

1

Memories of an African Sun

I grew up in an Africa that no longer exists. You can't go there. I can't go there. I lived there half a century ago, at the cusp of the modern age. We lived as missionaries on an outpost a hundred miles on dirt roads from the first town that had electricity, far out in the African wild lands, in the bush country.

At night, I would sit on the step of our house and watch the huge African sun start to sink behind the mountains surrounding us. Night after night I would sit and watch, as one by one across the vast scope in front of me I saw the village fires in the mountains and on the savannah spark to life in every direction. Then, moments later, a drumbeat would sound, first from one direction and then another. Some so distant, others close.

Into darkness the sun dropped, its passing bringing the hope of coolness. And I was left with the night and the sound of drums, and the light of fires cutting the darkness of the hills.

It was a different life from the one I live now. Fording rivers, reading by lantern, hauling water. Watching my mother make our bread and much of our food from scratch. Watching her teach and care for the people around us—people that she loved, and who also loved her, until her dying day.

So many mornings I woke to the sound of my father's voice on the veranda, teaching Africans in this remote outpost what had taken him years of college degrees in America to learn. He taught it freely and lovingly. For me, his voice remained always intertwined with the sun that came through my windows, as that light that defined so much of life rose again. Many days, except for the light from our lanterns and fireplace, we slept when it went down and woke when it rose.

Our African friends taught us much. Africa itself taught us much before it passed into this modern age. Africa defined my childhood.

In the pages that follow are my memories, and the lessons learned and lived. And woven through the thoughts and memories resides the memory of an African sun...

2

Packing

There are moments in our lives when a single event becomes the symbol that the entire trajectory of our life has suddenly changed. For me, it was mid-afternoon after a long bus ride, when I arrived home from third grade one day and found that our entire hallway and living room were filled with large, gunmetal black barrels that had been designed to hold crude oil on a transatlantic oil freighter ship. It's not what a child expects to find in the living room.

My yellow tin lunch box, in the shape of a school bus, was still in my hand as I weaved my way between the barrels, feeling ever so much smaller than they were. Large, round metal lids were in stacks against a wall. My mother was lining the barrels with heavy plastic sheets, and it appeared we were to pack up our household items in them.

Instead of the crude oil they had been designed for, these barrels filled with our belongings would be sealed with an airtight gasket, and taken back onto a freighter for the trip across the Atlantic, then on to meet the Indian Ocean and finally to rest at the Cape of Good Hope. Then they would be transported by trucks hundreds of miles north into the bush country of Rhodesia. We would not see them again for many months, long after we ourselves had arrived.

We would need to pack everything necessary to set up basic housekeeping: plates, silverware, sheets, towels. I remember putting a few of my toys in the black cavernous barrel and feeling like they were disappearing forever. In some ways they were because when I once again pulled them out, months later, I was in a very different state of mind.

I had heard the talk about "going to Africa" with only a vague understanding of the meaning of any of the discussions, or of where that might be. But now, as the afternoon sun shone through the open windows and bounced off the metal lids, as furniture was pushed further to the side and out of the way, as each second passed, that phrase became starkly real.

We lived in a time and place when traveling significant distances was a major endeavor. Interstates were in their infancy, only a few had been built—certainly none around us—and cars, while certainly spacious, did not have many of today's amenities, except for a local station on the radio. Most people, at least in our area of East Tennessee, were frugal with their money. They did not frequently jump in cars or planes and travel all over the country. Yet here we were, putting our belongings in huge empty oil barrels. Heading off to somewhere very far away.

I had seen the pictures of the buzzards on the houses in northern Ghana, brought back after my father and a pioneer missionary had flown into the country to survey the possibility of setting up a mission. I'd shaken my head with a mixture of horror and fear at the sight of those poor buzzards. I did not want to go there, thank you. And, I had seen the picture of my father, surrounded by laughing, friendly people and deep green tropical plants, drinking coconut water straight from a coconut in Ghana. That's all I knew of the continent we were going to. Nothing made sense. Nothing looked normal in the pictures. But I think it was the huge oil barrels in the living room that brought it all home—reality was setting in, and I wasn't sure I liked it.

It took some days for my parents to decide what could be taken—what would survive the arduous journey on the other end. Neighbors stopped in to take a look at the barrels. They were a novelty, made to go clear across the ocean and all, and having been constructed to carry oil and gasoline, which at that time cost around 20 or 30 cents a gallon. The entire trip across the ocean part sparked interest, as not many things were imported at that time. My mother would stop whatever she was doing during those days of packing and make coffee and chat with our visitors. She always seemed to have time for people.

I saw a picture the other day, at random, of an old rusting black oil barrel in an alley with a fire lit inside of it and homeless people gathered around it for warmth. I stood in the aisle of my local bookstore near the mall with tears streaming down my cheeks, rooted to the spot as I held the picture in my hands. I should have been crying for the homeless people—I know that—but at that moment all I could see was the old black barrels unexpectedly in our living room. Strange how we can so deeply associate an object with a feeling.

In my mind's eye, I see, long ago, a little girl putting a few toys in a huge oil barrel, not knowing for sure where it was going. And I feel all over again the uncertainty, the fear. I hear again the adults talking in the background… it seems children often hear adults talking as though they are in the background, their voices fading in and out, occasionally carrying random pieces of necessary information. They talked of fourteen injections, some painful, that I would take before we left—for inoculations against diseases I did not know existed. They talked of mosquito nets and their importance, and the quinine, or chloroquine, that I would need to start taking immediately and every week afterward for many years as a preventative against malaria, which was running rampant.

Those last days, I would often go outside and look at the ever-present Smoky Mountains that I loved. I would position myself on the top of the white wooden porch of our clapboard house and spin maple tree seedpods off of it, watching them slowly spin and glide downward to their new resting place. Or I would sit on the soft, brown and green needles under the beautiful, pungent, pine tree I had claimed as my own.

Then I'd walk along the lane, eating delicious honeysuckle that I pulled off as I made my way down the unpaved road. Or go over to the pond with my friends and gather a few more tadpoles to put in glass jars filled with pond water. Poor things, we always put them back in the pond but not before we had completely disrupted their environment.

Eventually, like clockwork, I would hear my mother, calling out from the window, for me to stay away from the stray dog I was trying to befriend. So I would go down to wade in the creek, and look up at Rattlesnake Mountain, and wonder if anyone had seen a snake up there recently.

But it was ending. I knew it. The freewheeling enjoyment of all those things was coming to an end. Change had arrived. It was stepping closer to me every minute.

Anyone who has ever gone through change, whether good or bad, will know what I mean.

I could feel it in the air.

Sometimes there is only one thing to do. At least it's the only thing I know, even now—hold on to God. And go forward. Always forward.

———ç———

Dear God, the changes of life start when we are young, and they continue. And yet, isn't life about that? About always going forward and trusting. I pray for myself, and for each of us, that we will understand that no day is like any other. Each is filled with something new, something else to know and something to learn.

7

Give me eyes to see that every day and every season is a time to grow in You, and to realize that like the psalmist says, my times are in your hands (Psalm 31:15).

3

Leaving Home

The propeller jet waited on the runway for its flight to New York City. We stood close together as a little family group at the silver-colored metal gate, on a cold but clear day in early February, waiting until the last possible moment. Above us, on the balcony of the airport, a large crowd had formed. Friends, colleagues from the schools where my father had taught and members from area churches stood alongside my mother's huge extended family. Their faces were alternately somber and excited or crying. My aunts, lined up at the balcony railing together, had on their best winter coats and hats.

But the worst of the pain was there at the runway gate. My two older brothers were staying behind. I was being taken away from them.

My last glimpse of home was of my oldest brother's wife sobbing, her dark hair buried in the coat of her baby girl in her arms. My brothers stood side by side, watching us. Later that day, my brother Jim, barely in college, would return to our empty home—standing cavernous now—and sit in the empty rooms and cry. Alone.

I think we all felt alone. For me, the impossible had happened. A family was torn apart. Not torn apart because of lack of love. Not torn apart spiritually. But torn apart geographically. At my mother's funeral a few years ago, the speaker asked God to bless my family for what we sacrificed. I appreciated that mention, yet I felt so aware of those who went before us. Who sacrificed for Africa to hear the gospel in ways I cannot imagine. Who bled for Africa. Who loved it and its people with their own lives.

Early missionaries to Africa took their wooden coffins with them. They had them built in New England or Britain, and the coffins traveled alongside them on the boats they sailed to Africa. Old names. Famous names of magnificent people, now only in history books. They knew they would not be coming back.

Except for those who immediately turned back upon arrival, only a few made the return trip home. If disease did not bring them down within months (black water fever, malaria and a host of other diseases ravaged systems which had no immunity at all), then hardship would simply overtake them.

Moravian missionaries had already arrived in Africa by 1737. In 1799, a mission society was formed in Britain with the intention of sending missionaries into the interior of Africa, and they did so by 1815. It was in 1855 that the fearless anti-slavery Scottish missionary explorer David Livingstone first explored the Zambezi River, and by the mid-1800s other groups of Scottish missionaries had also arrived.

In 1910, former American president Theodore Roosevelt traveled to Africa. Though he mercilessly slaughtered a staggering number of African animals while on safari, he nevertheless did manage to convince the ruthless Belgian government to unblock the entry of American doctors and nurses who were trying desperately to get into the Congo. He persuaded that government to allow an American medical mission station in colonial Congo. Those early missionaries built and ran hospitals and schools. They clothed and fed many. One can only lightly follow in such footsteps. They are very big footsteps.

Fifty years after those missions in the Congo were established, we found ourselves on our way to a new world. And yet also an ancient one.

For me, the depth of the meaning of the word *home* was being re-arranged—partly shattered, yet partly being built up to a solidness previously unimagined. I stood by that small propeller jet on the runway and turned back one last time to see them all before we boarded. The picture of them standing there, watching us leave, remains embedded in my mind to this day. Tears were falling everywhere.

I can't remember much beyond that. I had on a blue coat. My mother had on her red coat. That seems to be all I could see until we were well on our way. On our way to a place so far beyond my little imagination that there were no words.

Africa had called.

My father quoted one Scripture many times over the years until it was emblazoned in my mind.

During the night, Paul had a vision of a man of Macedonia standing and begging him, 'Come over to Macedonia and help us.' After Paul had seen the vision, we got ready at once to leave for Macedonia, concluding that God had called us to preach the gospel to them (Acts 16:9,10).

It's a Scripture I don't hear quoted much anymore.

The apostle Paul had a night vision. A call from the people of Macedonia, so he went.

My father felt a call from the people of Africa.

Is God calling you somewhere? It may be to the apartment or the house next door on your own street. So often, we look for what we consider to be the big thing, while stumbling and tripping over every other important situation that God has placed in our lives. The call to go to Egypt, to America, to Zimbabwe, to New York, to Illinois, or to next door is all the same call.

It's the call to show the love of God. And the time is now.

———✦———

Lord, place deep in our hearts the knowledge that we only have today to serve You, to be available to You. Wherever we are, at home or far from home, we place our times in Your hands. Whether You have given us a long life on a homestead or called us to places far and wide, we give it to You. Give us courage. Give us light. Give us perseverance. And give us success on Your behalf.

4

Night Flight

Pan American Airlines was a pioneer in transatlantic flights. Flight attendants were sophisticated, multilingual and had impeccable manners. The planes themselves were beautifully maintained. Some say that the Pan Am cuisine was inspired by the famous French restaurant, Maxim's de Paris. Perfect prime rib, lobster and lovely desserts were all served with great class.

Airline travel for the general public was still a novelty. It was far removed from the current era when thousands of planes cross the sky each day and people jump on board to visit relatives or for work, or to vacation a few states away. In those days, one still dressed for the occasion; all the passengers were wearing their best suits and beautiful dresses. So were we, me still in my blue tweed coat, my mother in her red coat with the soft fur collar and soft leather gloves, and my father in his fine black overcoat and city brimmed hat. We were not rich, but we had worn our best.

There is no way now to portray what it meant to board a huge, newly created Boeing 707 back then, in preparation for a transatlantic flight. The days are gone. The era is over.

We boarded the Pan Am flight in the evening on a clear New York City night. I can still remember the bright lights everywhere and the meticulous attention to detail from the airport ground personnel around the plane.

I can remember the sheer awe.

People coming to the United States from France or England in those days almost all still took an ocean liner. Few boarded the giant Boeings. Many of the missionaries we would soon be meeting had taken their voyage to Africa by freighter ship and had ridden in trucks or large four wheel drive vehicles inland from the coast. But here we were, climbing the steps to the magnificent monstrosity, barely able to see the stars for the blinding airport and runway lights everywhere. I felt, at the time, that we were taking our lives in our hands.

The plane left land behind within minutes and crossed the New York Harbor. Slowly the darkness overtook us. Once I saw another plane far in the distance in the dark sky, but other than that, for hours on end, we were in sheer darkness. Looking below, I asked my father what the tiny pinpoints of occasional light were on the vast dark surface. Ocean liners, he said. Or freight vessels. The lights were so small; I could not fathom how high up we were. The charming stewardesses provided clean, freshly laundered blankets, and fresh-smelling pillows to lie on. There were plenty of open seats on the plane and I was allowed to lay across an entire row. The darkness around me was profound.

In the darkness, long ago, Joseph woke Mary and the baby to flee for their lives. The wise men, warned in the night of danger, hurried back another way. Daniel waited in the lions' den through one long and dangerous night. David ran through the night from the murderous Saul.

And it was that same David, perhaps quoting the ancient prophet Moses, who had also had his share of night flights, who wrote, *You will not fear the terror of night* (Psalm 91:5).

Night Flights.

Perhaps there has been a time for each of us when we awakened in the depths of the night, worried and wondering. Or a night when we've had to get up with a sick child and rush to the emergency room to combat high temperatures. Or a phone call came from an aging parent or neighbor and in the darkness we hurried out to our car to reach them. There is something about the night that adds seriousness and urgency. Sometimes even clarity. We have realizations.

It was on that flight, so high above the dark ocean, that I finally understood, deep within myself, that East Tennessee and the people and places I so loved were going to be very far away for a very long time. I was flying into the unknown. Full speed ahead.

The sun would rise on London as we set down on the tarmac, and the world—my world—had changed. Irrevocably.

Father, be with us through the night watches. Help us on the night flights, when we go out in the night to places unknown, or to a hospital or a friend's house. Or if we wake in terror and trembling at the thought of the unpaid bills and the fear of a lost home. Or if we awake, unable to sleep, in sheer anticipation of a new and unknown life change—a wedding, a birth, a trip. Keep us safe through the nights of our lives, and give us courage, steadfastness, and even joy in the night seasons... to face the rising sun.

5

Why Did You Bring Me Here?

We stopped for weeks in Belgium to help a young church there and then again in southern Italy to give some missionaries the chance to go home. So it took us some time before we eventually arrived in Rhodesia. I did my schoolwork by correspondence in the various homes we stayed in or by the light of a table lamp at night in hotel rooms. My mother mailed my schoolwork papers in from wherever we were in the world during those months.

Our plane landed in the capital city of Salisbury, now called Harare, one late afternoon just as the sun was beginning to set. The missionaries who met us at the airport took us right away to the hotel where we would stay the night. The hotel was certainly a nice enough one, but the main thing I recall, as I fell asleep on a cot on the floor was the voices of the missionaries talking with my parents about the plague of spiders currently going on at the mission station. I fell asleep that night, my first night in Africa, with that conversation sliding along with me into my dreams.

Early the next morning, we set out for the long trip south into bush country. We left the city, drove by smaller towns and then left all towns behind us as we went further and further south. We drove hundreds of miles, eventually leaving behind, one after the other, the trappings of civilization as I understood it.

Electricity disappeared in the distance behind us. Paved roads were replaced with dirt ones, and finally with ones that were only dirt tracks that had been cut through the underbrush. We were headed toward the Native Reserve Land, later to be named the Tribal Trust Lands, where hundreds of thousands of Africans were being forced to live on the lands that were left to them by the colonists, who had taken the best for themselves. The Tribal Trust Lands were to be our home also.

The question that most went through my mind as I watched the scenery around me change and the trappings of civilization fall was, *What is happening to my life?*

It was only later that I realized that civilization had not fallen behind me. Only the familiar had fallen, and that is a very different thing, and not as serious.

Civilization is a way of behaving. Or should be. It's a way of thinking, a way of treating people. And it wasn't gone. The people consigned to the Tribal Trust Lands would treat me well indeed. I just didn't know it yet.

East Tennessee is a long way from the interior of Africa,

especially as it existed half a century ago. East Tennessee I understood—I was born there. I understood the Appalachians, the rivers, the small towns and the countryside. The way my large extended family spoke, and the way they thought. My mother's family had lived in those hills for generations. I understood the undertones. It made sense to me.

But Africa didn't.

Not at first.

I felt like Abraham, the patriarch, when he said, *I am a foreigner and stranger among you* (Genesis 23:4).

I cried endlessly on our first night at the bush mission station. I lay sobbing into the pillow on the small wooden bed that had been put into a corner of one of the verandas. When my mother came to try to comfort me, I had only one question of her as I lifted my hurting and angry eyes up from my tear-soaked pillow: *"Why did you bring me here?"*

But unexpectedly, something changed—and it was something inside of me. Africa, especially the Africa back then, had a wildness that made its way into my heart. A wildness that called out to me, on deep, dark, yet starlit nights. It called from the ground itself. And from the sound of drums as dusk fell.

I gazed at herds of buffalo that stretched all the way to the horizon. I felt the power of elephants stampeding after us, the ground shaking as we raced ahead. I sat by village women, far out in the bush, pounding maize on stone slabs, singing and talking as they worked. I met wonderful people from those villages. I stood atop enormous, high balancing rocks and looked out over a wild, windswept country, where there were no buildings for miles and miles on end, as far as the eye could see.

An understanding went deep into my heart. Did I forget Cherokee Lake or the town square with the white-steeple church building where my father had preached? Did I forget Sunday dinner with heaping mounds of mashed potatoes and pot roast—the best southern food you'd ever want to taste? No, I didn't forget. Like my mother, I loved it so much, from my very heart. But Africa also spoke. And redefined my life.

Are you somewhere in life that you wish you weren't? Are you crying out to God in agony, "Why did you bring me here?" Is it a divorce or death, or a move to a city you don't understand and don't like? Is it a fractured relationship with a friend? The loss of a house? The loss of a job?

It is not the circumstances that end up defining us. It's our response to the circumstances that do.

The challenge for each of us on this sometimes-rocky road of life is to stay close to God and to be as wise and strong as we can in our responses to those circumstances.

Although it may start out with "Why?" the circumstance that seems so difficult now may be the very one that later gives you a depth, wisdom, and understanding you would not otherwise have had.

As the prophet Isaiah once wrote, *Behold, I will do something new, Now it will spring forth; Will you not be aware of it? I will even make a roadway in the wilderness, Rivers in the desert* (Isaiah

43:19 NASB).

May this be so for you.

Father, give me the ability of Abraham, to venture into the new with You. Whatever form the new takes, whether a place or a way of thinking, give me courage to face what is ahead of me, courage to not be fearful of the unknown. Let me put my hand into Your hand, and let me feel Your safety, which is better than any safety the world can offer. Let the words of Jesus sink deep into my soul: Lo, I am with you always...

6

More to Come

On my first morning on our mission station, my father had gone off walking down a dirt road with some men to tour the station. My mother and I were in the front room of the stone and brick house at the top of the hill, with the family we were to stay with for a while. The house was surrounded with breezy wooden verandas and walkways, and the room we were in had long windows and a rustic stone fireplace. People were stopping by that morning to greet us—the same ones who had been waiting for us on a large stone terrace when we arrived the afternoon before were now making their way up the hill, to greet us again.

Suddenly two young boys came racing in, breathless. A long, dangerous python had just been seen lying on the path outside the house, heading straight toward the foundations, on the dirt path beside what would, a year later, be my own bedroom in that house.

Our hostess jumped up, and the next thing I knew she was standing in front of the fireplace with rifle in hand. With one swift action, she loaded it, walked outside—my mother and I behind her—and took aim. She blew that snake apart in one masterful move. Direct aim. Direct hit. It lay motionless, blown in half, on either side of the path. She turned, went back in, put the rifle back in its place and asked a couple of children to go gather the two halves of the snake and dispose of it. Then she proceeded to make tea for the group.

I was in shock.

It was the Wild West and something else, something I did not know the name for, all rolled into one.

What I experienced that morning was the tip of an iceberg. A large one. After watching this event unfold suddenly before my eyes, I could only wonder what else was ahead.

And there was so much more to come.

I would ride through the bush in Land Rovers, with no roads—not even dirt ones—to guide us. I would be chased by a troop of wild baboons, running as fast as I could. I would learn to carefully check my shoes for scorpions each morning, and sleep with dangerous spiders under my bed. I would be surrounded, alone, in the middle of a herd of wild hippos on the Zambezi River. I would stand in waist-high golden elephant grass as it swayed in the wind, knowing that lions could be somewhere nearby.

The wild part of Africa that I had landed in would become a massive adventure, an unheralded, unsought adventure of magnificent proportions.

I didn't know any of that then, that first morning. I only knew that at this station we apparently kept a long rifle someplace and took it out to blow apart large and dangerous snakes. And that the lady in front of me, who seemed somewhat motherly, was also a crack shot. It was enough for that one hour.

The next hour would hold its own new thought, like the discovery that due to drought we were not to always have running water. And the next hour …

I sometimes think that God doesn't show us everything to come because it would be hard for us to handle. People generally make that statement in a fatalistic way, thinking that the negative would be hard to handle, and that can be true. But the positive would be too. It's because we are creatures, like all beings on this planet. Like the birds, like the animals. Creatures who must walk through time, who must gather for this day, who must eat and work during this week. No matter what is to come, good or bad. We live in the present tense.

So there I sat, in front of a stone fireplace with what seemed to me like a still smoking gun in the house. And, through the open doors to my side, a morning sun rose over a savannah that was mildly terrifying in its expanse.

But what I also knew was ahead, on that first morning, was that I was with people who cared about me. That I had two parents who would literally have died for their children, if need be. And I was one of those children. This new place around me did not appear safe. Not to me, anyway. And yet, there was safety. All I had to do was look at the faces of those gathered in that room, strangers for the moment, but the community and the companionship in their faces were palpable even then.

And maybe this is what we most need to face the future. Hope and Community.

Hope that we do have a God, who cares about us, was willing to die for us and has not forgotten us, even in a strange land. And Community, the people who are in it with us. Who care in ways that matter—not just in words.

Because there is always more to come. Even when we die. More to come… forever.

God, I thank You that there is more to come. I thank You that through all of it You will be there with us. We have not been forgotten here, though at times we feel it. Give us the ability to stay in our present without needing to know every single step that is ahead. Because we already know what is most important—that You are there.

7

Our Daily Bread

———————— ⌇ ————————

Later that morning, I wandered into the kitchen, still suffering from my fitful night of sleeplessness, and happened upon an interesting scene in progress. My mother and our missionary hostess, the one who had shot the rifle earlier that morning, were engaged in an unusual drama that I watched with great and horrified interest.

"I so didn't want you to see this yet, Mary," the woman was explaining kindly to my mother, "not on your first day. I meant to have this done before you came in this morning."

My mother was staring strangely at the sifter in the woman's hands. She had been sifting flour from a big bin, and there were small bugs crawling around in the sifter. Weevils. My mother's eyes locked with the other woman's. I looked back and forth between them. I could only hope this meant we were leaving to go home as this venture was clearly not going to work out.

"They get in the bin every night," the woman continued,

and my eyes grew wider. The kitchen was a buzz of activity, the already hot sun streaming through the back door. "There's really nothing we can do. We've tried everything. So we just carefully sift each morning before we make the day's bread ..." Her voice drifted off.

I have no idea what transpired as the discussion continued. I only thought two things as I stood there in that hot kitchen. One, I wondered if we *could* somehow still back out of this endeavor.

And two, as I looked at her standing there, I realized that my mother must be a brave woman. I felt a strange security being near her right then. Somehow, her stoic acceptance of this—yet another of many strange new facts out in the middle of nowhere—made it seem clear that we would survive.

My mother continued asking questions... questions I did not want to know the answers to... and their voices faded behind me as I wandered on to see what other surprises the house might hold.

I have a great number of stories like that about food, but they not only don't tell the whole story, they don't tell the *real* story.

The food I ate at that mission station was healthier, as it turned out, than what many of my peers in America were downing at the time. There were few snack foods available to me—no Twinkies, no processed foods. There were no fast food hamburgers and no candy shops.

Much of what we ate we made, like the bread with the

weevils sifted out; or what was grown, such as vegetables from our gardens; and fruits from the trees around us, like guava and mangos. The women on that mission station also often put their heads together and produced magnificent potlucks for us all, and on Sundays after church we had afternoon tea together as a group.

On the reserve, there was a small brick building where sacks of maize, soap bars, kerosene, sardines, matches, teabags and the occasional sweets were sold by an enterprising young man. He had gained governmental approval, along with approval from a local Chief, to have his little one-room store and it was helpful to us more than once. He got the burlap sacks filled with maize from the government marketing board in charge of such things; the grain bags had apparently been allocated for the people on the reserve.

Someone had donated money for a pick-up truck for our mission Bible college, and every couple of weeks our driver made the long trip to the nearest town, Fort Victoria, and brought back canned goods, some bakery items, milk, and some meat. And when we made the trip into town ourselves we would bring back the same. There was also one small restaurant there that I so liked to go to. There was only one brand of chocolate bar that I knew of in the town, and sometimes I bought that.

One of the strangest things in life is that sometimes it is the absence of the very thing we think we are missing out on that ends up saving us. So many days, I went out in the late afternoon to pick myself a guava in the small orchard at the side of our yard. I climbed up to a tree branch, picked the fruit, and ate it in the faltering late afternoon sun. I had no idea at the time that I was being saved from a possible addiction to junk food because at that time I didn't understand the perils of it. I think back on those days, at times, and I can still see my hand reaching up for that fruit. There was something strangely idyllic about it. Whatever I missed by not being in on the newly burgeoning junk food craze at home, I made up for each and every day as I reached up my hand to that healthy alternative— my only alternative at the time.

I wonder if life with God is like that sometimes. We can look around and see what we are 'missing' in the way of sin or unhealthy lifestyles. Yet, we reach up our hand, over and over, for the good, for the healthy, for what God has said. And not at first, perhaps, but over time, we find that the good has become more powerful, that it has helped us in ways we might never have guessed. Until, finally, it's what we want.

I instruct you in the way of wisdom, says Proverbs 4:11, *and lead you along straight paths.* Sometimes we despair while on that path; we want what is not good for us. But over the long haul, what is truly not good for us, whether unhealthy, useless food or any other unhealthy thing, never seems to serve us well in the end.

It's easier when the sin or unhealthy choice is simply not available, as was true in my case back then. But even when it is, and we feel we are 'missing out,' the power of habit still wields its magic. Every day that we choose what is best for us is a day we are training ourselves.

I can guarantee you that freshly made bread, whether weevils had also once enjoyed the flour or not, and freshly picked guavas and mangos are better than chemical-filled food and candy. I didn't know that then, when I didn't even have very much in the way of candy, well-made or otherwise.

Isn't it odd, somehow, that I had to go to the heart of Africa to be safe from a world of sugar-laden, empty food?

Father, I pray for the empowerment to choose what is good and what is best for me, not what is just easiest or seems appealing at the moment. Protect me from myself when I seem to gravitate toward the lowest common denominator instead of allowing myself to be taught in your way of wisdom. Let me be a light to those around me, a light that shows a path to physical, spiritual, and emotional health. And provide for me those who can shine that light for me, too, in areas that I am weak.

8

A Medical Mission

We were a medical mission. The mission station itself had been started by New Zealanders who were intent on giving medical help and aid in those parts of Southern Rhodesia where none had previously existed. Their presence in the early part of the century had a profound effect, and they had engendered great love from many Africans in the bush. Some of the New Zealanders stayed for long years, some died early from sickness and others had to return home to New Zealand, ill and weakened from their years in the bush country. The New Zealanders had become overwhelmed with the vast needs in all of the tribal areas and issued an invitation for American missionaries to help them.

Early medical procedures were carried out by the first American doctor in a makeshift tent located under a large fig tree, surrounded by wire fencing to keep roving cattle out. An examination bed was set up inside the tent. Surgeries were performed on a wooden door laid out between two barrels.

Later, the early doctor and nurses were allowed to move their medical operations to a local Matsai clinic, which consisted of six large thatched huts. They worked long hours, and the lab work—such as the examining of specimens—was done by lantern light in one of the huts late at night.

But plans for an amazing hospital, far out in the middle of bush country, were underway, and hundreds of thousands of bricks were being made on-site. The hospital and the nursing school alongside it—which would be used to train medical assistants—was finished and dedicated just a few years prior to our arrival. Over four thousand Africans showed up for its dedication. Its first patient was a local Chief.

We had a large primary and secondary education branch at our mission, started by the New Zealand missionaries and continued by the Americans, that eventually served thousands of children from many miles around. Many of the adults on our mission station were capable teachers along with their other areas of professional expertise and responsibility. The students from our schools were known for their strong learning base, and a number were able to go on to even higher education. Arithmetic, geography, nature studies, domestic science, and many other subjects were taught in the schools. My father taught Latin to the upper secondary students. Massive gardens had been planted for food for the schoolchildren.

The amount of money that poured in from American churches to help the people living on the tribal trust lands of southern Africa was really nothing short of astounding. We were able to start a Teacher Training Program to which a huge number of individuals applied—there was a great desire on many people's parts to learn this professional skill that could be used to earn income. Many successful teachers were taught at our teacher training school.

We also had a Bible College, which is where my father came in. A year after our arrival he became the president of the college. He was a thoughtful intercultural teacher, and the students loved him. He taught so many long hours. Some of the Bible College students came from the Matsai Reserve, where we lived, but many also came from other parts of Zimbabwe and southern Africa. My father's classes were held on our front veranda because the area the college had previously been using had to be converted to the mission storeroom. The usual storehouse had caught fire and burned down. He taught both the Greek and Hebrew languages to his Bible College students, along with many other subjects. These students, who by that time already knew at least two and sometimes three languages, learned two more and learned them well, some later going off to distant universities and greatly excelling.

Each day my father broke for lunch, and I observed him, still on the veranda, teaching one man, in particular—an extremely bright man—who then turned around and used the rest of the lunchtime to teach my father *his* language, Shona.

The college students walked for miles to villages to preach on the weekends until we decided to use some of the mission money for each of them to have a bicycle for their weekend trips. They excitedly examined those brand new bicycles on the day they finally arrived. They were amazing men. Each one of their interesting and intriguing life stories would fill a book.

The centerpiece of our mission was the hospital, which sat at the front of our station. It was really a series of buildings connected by breezeways. In front of the wide entrance was a large open field. Herders marched their cattle across the field on their way to grazing grounds and back, and the sick and hurting would sit there while waiting to be seen. In a circle around that open space were our homes, and off to the side our many school buildings. A circular dirt road, side roads and an assortment of paths connected everything, and I could walk from the hospital in a huge circle to nearly every house, the ever-present cattle herders and their long-horned steers always in the middle of my journey. One could see the hospital, it seemed, from almost everywhere.

There were streams of tuberculosis and malaria patients and numerous women who gave birth in our hospital. Individuals were rushed in from far away with a wide assortment of emergency concerns: snake bites, which sometimes resulted in amputations; children with kwashiorkor, a disease stemming from protein-deficiency malnutrition; illnesses from parasites; infectious diseases such as measles, rabies, tumors, respiratory problems, gashes from cattle gores and crocodile and hippo bites. So many serious problems, and they all needed immediate intervention.

A dirt landing strip located at the far edge of our mission station, two miles from the mission itself, served as a small plane runway. It just sort of started at one point in the bush, went a little way and then ended. It basically went nowhere, just sat by itself like that. At times a plane from one of our other mission stations flew in with patients in need of medical treatment on board, and a pickup truck from the mission would travel the two miles to retrieve the patients and transport them by truck to our hospital. Or, one of the missionary bush pilots from elsewhere would land. At the beginning, the first doctor on our mission station had used a small plane to even get into the area at times—what passed as the way in was so bad. Those first, so-called dirt roads to the mission station were mostly just elephant grass that seemed to part here and there.

The medical staff performed many surgeries. Many of the patients walked or were carried in others arms, or came by ox cart for the long miles to get help, but sometimes we were able to bring patients in via one of our Land Rovers. In addition to the exceptional doctor who seemed to work day and night, we had a number of single nurses who gave up careers and took ships to travel to the bush country. One of our nurses had for years been in the U.S Air Force Nursing Corp. Our medical staff housed thousands of patients and cared for them. They led well-baby clinics and gave untold numbers of vaccinations. They were a cut above, and deeply overworked. I was truly amazed by what they managed to do, given what they had.

Our Bible College truck, which had been purchased with

donated funds for us to haul things in, was a big deal. Sometimes our driver drove the hundred miles over dirt roads to pick up supplies and one night when he did not return, people from the station, both missionaries and Africans, set out looking for him. When at last a group of Africans found him, the truck was overturned off the road. He was lying in a ditch some forty miles out in the bush, one of the long bones in his forearm sticking straight out into the air.

There was a knock on our door in the middle of the night as the Land Rovers arrived back at the station.

"Mr. Simkins, the doctor needs you to get your drill, bits, and screws down to the hospital immediately," a male voice said. It was the voice of one of the orderlies. Our doctor knew we had the exact drill he needed to use for the procedure. All of us on the station pretty much knew what each other owned. The doctor operated on our driver that night, using my father's drill and a metal plate to screw the bones back together. There are so many stories like this, of their heroics.

It has always struck me as odd that people create a dichotomy between miraculous healings, medical knowledge and traditional ethnic medicine such as herbs and salves from plants. As though each one was against the others somehow, in some sort of tug of war, instead of each being part of what God has provided.

Luke, the Gospel writer, was a doctor, and he does not appear to have renounced his profession upon becoming a believer. Paul, the apostle, is found telling his friend Timothy what to take for a stomach ailment (1 Timothy 5:23), while at the same time healing people of serious disease and suffering, with a near sweep of his hand. These treatment methods are not opposites as much of current culture would have us believe. It's like pitting a red sweater against a blue sweater. They are both sweaters, just different. One might put the red sweater on for a certain occasion, but the blue sweater may be more appropriate for another.

I have had the privilege of seeing people healed in miraculous ways through faith and prayer. I have also watched as doctors and nurses applied their long years of study to a situation and did the amazing art of medical intervention. And I have seen the herbs and tonics of alternative medicine—that knowledge learned through generations of trial and error—do wonders in rejuvenation and healing.

Each of these areas of healing has been misused. But things do not always need to be judged according to those who misuse them. If they were, we would be in trouble in every area of life. The point at which these healing routes converge in their best renditions is where I want to be.

I learned the value of this Scripture: *Every good and perfect gift is from above, coming down from the Father of the heavenly lights, who does not change like shifting shadows* (James 1:17).

God has given us many gifts of healing, and it seems we are often intent on squabbling over them. Perhaps the day we collaborate instead of arguing over the gifts we will begin to see a progress we have not yet known.

For us, back then? We were a medical mission, no doubt about that. We had a highly trained staff. But we also knew our way fairly well around the bush country when it was dangerous, and we knew how to live by faith.

———⌒———

Father, I thank You that You heal and that perfect gifts come from You. Teach me everything—how to eat right, how to live right, how to think right. Thank You for my brothers and sisters who have studied and learned medical knowledge and for those who have studied the ways of the wild medicine. Give us mental health and physical health. Give us a heart and mind that knows You can supersede all we know and reach into us with a magnificent healing power. Give us humility as we pray and as we search. Help us to honor the fact that so many of us are trying to help others find health.

9

Community

———————⚶———————

One of the first things I learned upon arriving at our mission station was that we were a community. Not in an idealistic or abstract sense, but in the concrete sense that we depended on each other in a real way. The survival of our station depended upon contribution by its members and upon cooperation and friendship.

I had been fortunate to come from a place, Johnson Bible College, in Tennessee, where the strains of the music of community already played strong in my mind. Located in Appalachian country, with a dairy farm at its center for income, the school had a motto that anyone who would work at manual labor and contribute their efforts could come to school even if they couldn't pay, so I had a strong foundation for the concept of community.

All the children and teenagers at the station called every adult other than their own parents aunt or uncle. My parents were suddenly Aunt Mary and Uncle Cyril. But the feeling of family and community ran deeper than verbal acknowledgment.

These were the people we went to when something happened in the middle of the night. These were the people who would put out fires if they sprung up, brought food to the sick, saved us from snakes that made their way into our house, who loaded up Land Rovers and went to look for anyone who was lost. They had us over for dinner over and over, shared with others when they didn't have enough and helped repair the truck. There was simply no one else.

Stripped of some of the trappings of modern civilization, people were the key, and we banded together—for survival and purpose. We understood the value of the people, both in the villages around us and on our mission station.

Many of the adults at our station were experts in their own right in their particular fields of study, and they pitched in to teach us children. My father taught history to some of the older grades and the pharmacist who had come to work at the hospital to support the doctor and nurses taught science. He also taught me how to play the piano.

I learned how to sew from the doctor's wife—a delightful, dear, petite woman at our mission. Once a week, during the hours when the electricity was on, my mother sent me down to her house, and for three hours she showed me how to carefully cut patterns, use her sewing machine and proudly smiled at the dresses and skirts I managed to produce. Her little kitchen was warm and fragrant as we made sugar cookies together after some of our sewing lessons.

My art teacher was the pharmacist's wife. A fine artist herself, she was also generous with time and effort as she taught our class to draw. She would set out various pieces of clay pottery or flowers and show us how to think in artist's terms. With her dark head bent over her work, she explained how to hold the brush, create depth and shade. I personally did not turn out to be anyone's prize student in art. To my dismay, I could barely draw, but the art teacher's efforts gave me a great appreciation for the art that others could amazingly produce. I held onto my best piece of work, a clay water pot drawing, for many years.

The children and teenagers on our station were also put to work—real, meaningful work. Some were taught to do significant medical tasks at the hospital, and they were a great help to the doctor and nurses. One learned to help keep the generator running. Another helped draw up construction plans for a building. They carried out numerous chores and tasks around the mission. The older ones could drive Land Rovers through the bush, and later some learned to fly small planes. Their exploits were daring. Sometimes we got into trouble. Many were skilled trackers and hunters and highly adept at understanding their way through the bush country for days on end. They were risk-takers.

The children on that mission station, and at our other mission areas, were hardy. It's the word that always comes to mind when I think of them. I don't know if they innately started out that way or if they just grew to be that way due to our circumstances, but the stamina, and sheer, undiluted grit that they showed impressed me then and impresses me now. Their adventures and tales would fill volumes.

For a long time, I wondered why it was that I turned out to be such an individualist since I was raised in so many strong community environments. Then it finally dawned on me that the communities I grew up in were, in fact, part of the reason.

In a good community, everyone counts and is counted on. Individuals matter and are taught to carry their own weight. These days, the word *community* sometimes seems to connote some notion of other people doing things for you, of you not having to work quite as hard. Yes, the sharing of talents is part of a community, but in the communities I grew up in, it was not so much about what a person would get out of others as it was about everyone doing their own part and making things work. It was about going above and beyond. Somehow, it created in me a paradoxical combination of individualism and a strong sense of how my decisions and actions affect the whole.

I sped around the mission station many days on my treasured Raleigh bicycle. I rode until the paths around the station and to nearby villages simply ran out, and there were only bushlands left. My bicycle had a tire pump, tire patches, a spanner and assorted other tools strapped here and there—I learned early that riding a bike in the bush meant being prepared. Often, I rode with my pet chameleon on my arm, flying across the dirt roads of our station. I have no idea if the chameleon enjoyed these daring rides, racing along with me as the air rushed in our faces, but in retrospect, I imagine he did not. He clung on valiantly, though, until we returned home.

There is an African proverb, so old that there are many variations of it, that says in essence that it takes a village to raise a child. It was true on our mission station, and it was true in the villages we lived among.

We don't forget people with whom we shared a singular adventure. The ties that bind us to those with whom we experienced great things are strong.

I was lucky. I was fortunate to ride my Raleigh from person to person on the circle dirt road and learn such an assortment of things. Personally, I think this is a little piece of what Jesus was getting at when He said to His disciples, *Let the little children come to Me* (Luke 18:16). The disciples had been sending the children away so "important" things could be done. If our communities and our cultures are too busy to stop, teach and take care of the children wandering among us, then what are we really accomplishing?

What are we possibly creating if we have missed being the communities who stop and hear the children?

God, help me to always have the time and the energy for children, for what is a community if it misses being there for its littlest or its oldest members? Help me to find ways to create community around myself that includes them, and to support everyone else who is doing that as well. Please stop me when I think any activity is more important than they are. Help me always remember that the Lord I serve stopped everything to be with the children.

10

Gratitude

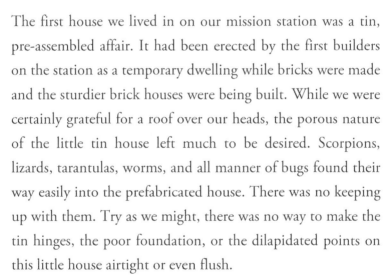

The first house we lived in on our mission station was a tin, pre-assembled affair. It had been erected by the first builders on the station as a temporary dwelling while bricks were made and the sturdier brick houses were being built. While we were certainly grateful for a roof over our heads, the porous nature of the little tin house left much to be desired. Scorpions, lizards, tarantulas, worms, and all manner of bugs found their way easily into the prefabricated house. There was no keeping up with them. Try as we might, there was no way to make the tin hinges, the poor foundation, or the dilapidated points on this little house airtight or even flush.

Give thanks to the Lord, the Bible says repeatedly.

But how hard sometimes.

Modern science is confirming what common sense has told us for a long time—that simple gratitude is one of the most profound and energizing of all emotions. It turns the mind to new horizons, rejuvenates the soul and lifts the spirit to a lighter place. We don't even have to start out by trying to be grateful for difficulties. Just learning to be grateful for the meal in front of us, for a running car or for a child waking up healthy—if we truly feel it, this kind of gratefulness can change everything.

It was in our little bug-ridden house that I learned this profound lesson.

One particular day brought dozens of scorpions running across our floors. I stood on the old sofa in the living room sobbing as they ran in every direction underneath me. My parents tried their best to get the scorpions out of the house, and then after a good long time of their comforting me, I settled down with a book, relatively secure. It began to rain, a welcome sound after the months of heat. The large drops echoed off the tin roof. My mother sat with my father in the living room and shared tea. "Cyril, when it's all said and done, and we get back to America, in a house of our own, do you think we could have a little porch? You could put a tin roof on it. You and I could sit out there together like this, drink tea and listen to the rain."

Where do you go to get that kind of life spirit? How do you learn to be grateful?

By starting with the smallest thing in front of you. Even if it means having to close your eyes and only listen to the beautiful sound of the rain as it hits an old tin roof.

We find what we look for. Today, look for gratitude. Look

for one thing, no matter how ordinary, to be grateful for. Even if you have to close your eyes and simply listen. Or remember. Or hope for.

———— ∽ ————

Father, give me a heart of gratitude. Not of made up, superficial gratitude but of true gratitude and thankfulness. Help me understand in my heart of hearts what it means to have food to eat, a bed to sleep in and a roof over my head. Help me let go of greed and self-pity. Show me a good and right way to live in this world. Let gratitude, one of the greatest of emotions, become part of my character and spill out from my life to all those around me.

11

Spiders and Snakes

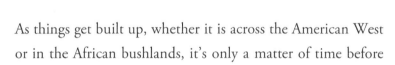

As things get built up, whether it is across the American West or in the African bushlands, it's only a matter of time before humans take over, and the wildlife, insects and snakes are pushed further and further to the side.

But before that happens, there is a long period where it's more accurate to say that the humans are living in the abode of the animals and insects, not the other way around.

That is where we found ourselves on our mission station. They had been pushed nowhere back then. We felt quite successful if the snakes and the spiders were pushed back a few inches from the house.

Behind our house, at the end of our station, there was a clearing where the dirt road that went around nearly the entire station ended, right there on the hill where our house sat. Beyond the clearing was a gorgeous splash of subtropical plants and trees, followed by a burst of brilliant red poinsettias tumbling wildly down over many rocks. Frangipani trees scattered around a path that descended off the hill to eventually start up again as the road. It was not a sculptured garden, just trees and plants winding their beautiful and riotous way across the ground, down the rising hill behind us and here and there around the house.

Flowering trees and plants bombarded us when the rains fell. Rock walls had been built in a couple of places—someone's attempt to keep the bush at bay from the gushing flowers but not always successfully. Beyond the walls, the bush completely took over, interspersed with the famous rocks of Zimbabwe jutting their way through the underbrush. The underbrush was thick, the trees were close and paths wandered off to various locales or just eventually petered out altogether as the bush took over. My natural love of adventure was in high gear—I explored those areas, far and wide, both on my own or with friends, and sometimes got lost. I liked to lie high on top of a rock formation, resting from an excursion down a long footpath, watching and waving to the villagers below.

After school, I would often sit on one of the prehistoric-looking granite rock slabs to the side of our house, waiting for the legavaan I had befriended to come out and sit beside me to sun himself. A legavaan is a type of rock monitor lizard. They can grow to six feet long and up to thirty pounds and they look somewhat like an iguana. He never hurt me as we sat there together though I've heard since that sometimes they bite quite ferociously.

There were many green and black mambas near our house. More than once we found one happily sunning himself on our screened-in veranda in the morning or afternoon. It was unnerving because a mamba's bite can kill within minutes. One family found a cobra wound under their bedsprings. They had heard movement under the bed during the night and got up to discover the snake. Apparently cobras like to go into houses to escape the heat, mostly in barely developed areas, which is certainly where we were.

I stood behind our house one afternoon watching a spitting cobra dangle from a tree limb. He was as long as the similarly colored grapevine dangling beside him, and he was eyeing me, which was scary since a spitting cobra can spit its venom up to nine feet and aims for the eye of its prey, sometimes causing blindness.

A number of boa constrictors, puff adders and boomslang snakes were often seen around our home, in the bush, and on the mission station. I had a frightening run-in with a coiled Cape cobra, his hood spread out, poised to strike me. He was in the middle of his strike, my foot less than an inch from him, and he simply stopped mid-strike. It could only be God who protected me because almost nothing on earth is fast enough to escape the lightning strike of a poised Cape cobra.

I was afraid of the spiders. In the little tin house we lived in before moving to the top of the hill, we had many. When the chairman of the mission society came to visit—a rare occurrence for our mission station—my mother was so upset because the night before he arrived we found two tarantulas right where he was to sleep. A tarantula's poison can make a person very sick, but we had no real way to keep them out. One of my most vivid memories is of an enormous spider that looked like a naked baby bird crawling under my bed before I had to sleep there. We had no electricity at that point, only flashlights or kerosene lamps to look for it. We couldn't find it. It had most likely crawled high up into the bed frame. I had nowhere else to sleep, no place of escape. I lay in bed that night, staring at the darkness, tears streaming down my face.

You can go to the large cities of sub-Saharan Africa today and easily not see a single deadly spider or snake. You can even go on a sightseeing safari now and not be in any particular danger. It was different then, on our mission station, where we had to have guns in case a wild animal ventured near us and a hospital that specialized in crocodile and snake bites, as well as longhorn cattle gorings. Hippo attacks were not uncommon. We were situated just above the lowveld—a place that was, at that time, teeming with wild animals.

I think, though, that in our modern, technology-driven world, we must not be complacent. In the grandest, most high-rise penthouse in the world, there are things that are just as dangerous as a poisonous snake or a crocodile. Perhaps far more so.

As it says in Romans 1:30, there are actually people who are *inventors of evil.* What a horrifying thing. Jesus said not to fear those who can kill only the body, rather be concerned about what might land us in trouble eternally (Luke 12:4-5). True evil—not the venom of snakes and spiders—is what can destroy us forever. Death from a poisonous spider is a tragic loss of life, and certainly not the way the world was originally created to operate. But eternal fate from a poisonous, deadly evil of the spirit is far more fatal.

I learned something from those spiders and snakes. Yes, even from them. They taught me skills of observation while I walked in the bush. But something else ...

I learned that a person can't play around with deadly things. Deadly creatures kill. That is fact, not theory. And those deadly things are not just in the jungle or the bush country. Deadly things can also be spiritual, taking the life right out of a person. There are things not to try, things not to risk. Because it can be a matter of a very short window of time to attempt to reverse the effects.

Father, we pray as Jesus taught us—deliver us from evil. We pray for protection from all danger and particularly from the dangers contrived by the inventors of evil. Put Your shield of love and light around us, that the darkness of that danger will always pass us by, leaving us unscathed by its evil. You dwell in Light. Protect us with it.

12

Villages

———— ꝋ ————

Most everyone for many long miles around our mission lived in villages. A few individuals living closer to town had small, square, one-room homes made of cement, but by far the majority lived in thatched roof huts, with mud and cow dung floors. These floors were polished to shining beauty. The packed dirt area in and around the village was swept clear each and every morning. Any particle that might possibly attract an insect or snake was swept away until a clear, flat dirt surface remained. Those who had cement block houses also came out early with their brooms to sweep off the area in front of their home. There is something truly invigorating and pristine about that one action, somehow. Like a fresh start to the day, a new beginning.

The first night I slept in a hut, I was shocked at how cool it was. I didn't know why it was so cool, but no doubt it had to do with the ingenuity that went into building the huts. Upon arising, I found a container of fresh, cool water already prepared for me by the friends I was visiting, to splash on my face and wash my hands in. I emerged from the hut that morning just in time to be blasted by the red-orange sun as it lifted from the horizon, and I realized again just how cool and comfortable that hut had been. The coolness was surprising because the sunrise in progress was one of the largest I had ever witnessed, as that very hot orange globe rose over the Dewure River.

I have so often run up against the misconception that people living in those villages were somehow backward, uncivilized, and not as smart as others. Nothing could be further from the truth.

What is *uncivilized* anyway? Is it a man screaming in uncontrollable rage at a nearby car in a traffic jam on the L.A. freeway? Or an irate customer yelling irrationally at the service provider behind a coffee counter?

I found none of these sorts of behaviors in the villages near where we lived.

The people we lived among were as intelligent and bright as anyone anywhere else on earth. One thing that astounded me was their quick ability to pick up and learn languages foreign to their own. It seemed they did it in record speed. Their eagerness to learn was undeniable.

Our friends from surrounding villages had a great deal of knowledge that we didn't have. We depended on them at times for understanding the way of the bush, and we had much to learn. I can still see that sudden laughter and broad smile as yet another of my mistakes in dealing with the world around me unfolded.

There are numerous customs that pertain to village life, such as not entering a village unannounced, without making your presence known.

I used to sit and watch the women in nearby villages pound out maize as they chatted away. And I watched as the cattle were herded back at night into the kraal, an enclosed structure near the village.

I don't know what it is that makes people in some cultures assume that those in others are backward simply because they have different blocks of knowledge to work with. The people we knew in the villages around us were just like us, only culturally different, and with a different set of skills. Yes, we brought a lot of knowledge to them, helpful knowledge they told us, but they were fully capable of learning what we knew, just as we also could learn some of what they understood. When one culture knows something that another doesn't, anywhere in this world, it doesn't mean the second culture is not intelligent. It means that knowledge in a particular area is lacking. It could be highly valuable knowledge that is lacking, but that is still the subject at hand. Not intelligence.

The colonialists severely damaged Africa and her people. There is no way to make that fact any different than it is, and one of the damaging things was their pervasive belief, which they carried back to the West, that African people were somehow not intelligent. It was an evil lie that they perpetrated for many years. The African villagers of Zimbabwe that I lived among had some of the sharpest minds, brightest eyes, and kindest demeanors I have ever known.

I am not idealizing village life. Some of the people I knew were eager for a chance to change their circumstances; some were hoping for one of the few new cement homes. Or an education. Or land ownership. Or, simply, better times. Many were hoping real opportunity would knock.

Everywhere we went, in those days, we were warmly greeted by villagers walking on a path or sitting near their village. We were welcomed with a handshake, a smile and a friendly greeting and often by an interesting moment of conversation.

I liked to sit on one of the smaller granite rocks by the dirt path near the village closest to us, and wait for the headman from that village to come walking home, his three wives behind him. I was waiting for his third wife, walking behind everyone— a young girl of about seventeen —who had a grand, wide smile and beautiful face and used to wave eagerly to me as I sat on the rock, watching the afternoon fade away. She was generally balancing an enormous basket on her head, her body swaying in astonishing posture underneath. I am not sure why, but I think of her fairly often. She exuded a happy charm, she liked me, and I felt so blessed by her clear excitement at seeing me once again.

Growing up in a village does not in any way equal backwardness or ignorance. What I saw in those villages was a people like all other peoples.

It is somehow distressing to hear of the guided tours that many tourists are taking through villages set up on the tourist routes nowadays so that they can get "the village experience."

Villages are not stage shows. Africa is not a tourist performance.

Villages are where people live.

Whether a person lives in a high-rise in Hong Kong, a cardboard house in the slums of Rio, a farmhouse in Iowa or a home on a Native American reservation, people are the same. With a wide assortment of different cultural thoughts and different trappings, they remain the same. They want love. They want respect. They want to learn. Many crave education. They want safety for their children and families. Most want to be self-sufficient and not dependent on others. They want a livelihood. They want to understand truth. These are the traits that run through the veins of the human race, no matter where people are located.

Many of the people living in the villages around me those fifty years ago were Christians. The Christians of Zimbabwe are my brothers and my sisters. We are equally God's children. And I am so blessed because of it.

It was the apostle Peter who proclaimed... *I now realize how true it is that God does not show favoritism, but accepts from every nation the one who fears him and does what is right* (Acts 10:34-35).

I believe that.

Some days when I'm paying the outrageous electric bill to

run my central air conditioning, when I open windows to save money only to have the water-laden Illinois humid heat barrel in on me, I think back to that morning at Dewure, of emerging from my calm sleep in that cool, cool hut while the African sun was blistering its way up into the sky, heat waves already shimmering in the air, and I kind of wonder how they did it.

Probably some knowledge we don't have here yet.

———◇———

Father, help me to remember always that people everywhere want many of the same things that I do. They want safety for themselves and their children. They want a decent and productive way to make their living. They want provisions of food and shelter. They want to learn. They want respect. They want to hold on to the good cultural influences that have shaped them and that matter to them. Help each of us, everywhere, to hold onto the good and to let go of the wrong cultural influences, of wrong thinking, and to embrace Your ways. The ways of God… which are goodness, righteousness, love, and peace.

13

Mission Boxes

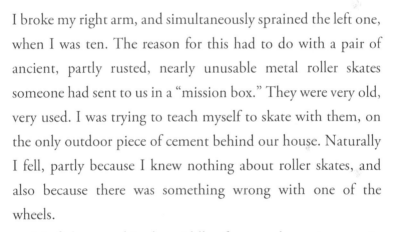

I broke my right arm, and simultaneously sprained the left one, when I was ten. The reason for this had to do with a pair of ancient, partly rusted, nearly unusable metal roller skates someone had sent to us in a "mission box." They were very old, very used. I was trying to teach myself to skate with them, on the only outdoor piece of cement behind our house. Naturally I fell, partly because I knew nothing about roller skates, and also because there was something wrong with one of the wheels.

My father stood in the middle of our yard, turning over in his hand the pair of miserable skates, examining them, shaking his head in silence, a strange look in his eyes.

And yet, I am acutely aware that my words risk sounding ungrateful to many ears. People will start in with stories of "making do." We did a great deal of "making do" on the mission field and didn't mind doing so. I have a very strong appreciation of the real value of making do and of the character it can form. I also know another reality... that when we give other people and their children things we wouldn't dare use ourselves, things that are dangerous (like chipped drinking glasses or lawn mowers that smoke) then we are running a risk of not caring from our heart about the people we claim we are helping. When people are in a famine, yes, they will eat anything, including dirt. We would too. But if we have the means to give them a bowl of healthy oatmeal or even send just the grain itself, it is much more caring than saying, "Maybe we could ship more dirt across the ocean to them. They appear to be eating it." What a strange way to think.

Occasionally, we would receive boxes of torn clothes, dirty shoes, coats (I have no idea why someone would send a heavy winter coat to the subtropics) and other nearly unusable, old items. I also have no idea why anyone would have wanted to spend money on the shipping. I think the Scripture in Luke 6:38 was lost to those individuals: *For with the measure you use, it will be measured to you.* Personally, I find this to be one of the most scary and thought-provoking Scriptures in the Bible. A Scripture worth long, long thought.

There is another side to this mission box story. We also received amazing boxes mailed from individuals who had taken time to either investigate the actual place we were or to write to ask what our needs were. People who sent items that we could purchase nowhere. I remember my mother's ecstatic delight when someone sent us some boxes of Jell-O. We had a refrigerator that ran off of kerosene at that time so we could actually make the Jell-O. And good clothes, sometimes not new and maybe not this year's fashion, but we didn't care at all about that because they were in such usable shape, clean and mended. It was a delight to open those boxes. It was truly a godsend when people took the time and energy to pack helpful items. Some sent new things they had found on sale, bought especially to just be kind and helpful. And, then there were the people who showered us with hundreds of beautiful clothes to simply give away to help the people around us. Their generosity was outstanding. Beautiful things to help so many that had so little. Bless them, bless them! Even today, I bless them.

Back to my skating injury. I was dutifully sent down to the hospital to have my aching arms examined. The medical staff was extremely busy that day, so I sat on a little stool with one of the nurses, in the center of the tuberculosis ward while she put the cast on. I can still see the black metal beds lined up in rows, the hot afternoon sun glinting off the hospital windows, with the many tuberculosis patients lying flat on their backs in the beds in the sweltering heat. In our part of Africa, tuberculosis was definitely not a thing of the past.

My broken arm got well, of course, and it turned into just another of the many scrapes and bruises of childhood. The old, outdated, damaged skates were thrown away, as they should have been in the first place.

But the message I learned stayed with me. When I give to

others, I'm deciding what will be given to me. Is that what the Scripture in Luke 6:38 means? It must be what it means. And I'm guessing it's not just the *thing* or the item I'm giving to others that is important, but the spirit and generosity in which I give it. Is that what the Scripture means? If someone knows that it means anything different, please let me know. Because it's the only way I know to read it.

Give, and it will be given to you... for with the measure you use, it will be measured to you.

Scary.

Father, create in me a giving heart. Don't let me turn a blind eye on the needs around me, or around the world. The condition of my neighbor's car, the yard they can no longer keep up, or the thousands of children, mothers, and families around the world who do not have their basic needs met. How exactly am I going to face You if I don't help? I pray that I will never get lost in subjects of economics or nationalism or politics or any vain reasonings, but will only believe Your word. I wonder if You will even care about mine or any other culture's excuses. Your word says that what I do in this area of giving impacts me personally. Oh, help me, Father.

14

My Teacher

Why would a beautiful, thirty-year-old single woman choose to leave everything, including a successful teaching career, and come to teach eight young American children in the middle of the African bush country? The only answer that I ever heard was the one that she herself gave—that she felt led by God to do so. I'm not certain that anyone else could quite understand unless it was the unmarried nurses also present at our station. They had done the exact same thing.

But the answer sufficed for the teacher. Before leaving America, she faced a number of people who argued that she was throwing her life away and that she would probably never marry since she would be stuck out in such a remote wilderness for years. They warned her of the terrible loneliness she would experience. All of their words seemed to roll off of her.

She was one of the most beautiful people I had seen, with glossy dark brown hair she wore short and wavy and gorgeous brown eyes with a cheerful glint. She was indefatigable, with a smile that lit up the room every morning. She was my teacher, and she had a gift—the ability to teach with almost nothing at hand. Whatever textbooks we had, they were not new though she made sure they were good. I think she must have brought some of them with her, but I never actually knew.

We learned about ancient Egyptian culture by gathering the African dirt, mixing it with water and making hand-formed pottery. Then we painted symbols on the sides to learn how hieroglyphics would have looked. We made all sorts of what we termed Egyptian objects for that unit—we were certainly surrounded with plenty of dirt for our creations. And as we molded our pottery, she talked of Pharaohs and the Nile. We had one globe in our classroom, and we slowly worked our way through many of the countries on it. We learned math with one textbook and lots of paper. She simply sat at our table with us and gave us the sums and over and over worked with us until we got them.

For the years I was at the station, I was the constant in the classroom. While I was there, two families and their children who had been living at the mission for some time moved to other parts of Zimbabwe, and one family returned to America. One of the families went to Fort Victoria and started a printing press. They printed song books in Shona and a large variety of other highly useful materials. There was the additional fact that some of the missionaries eventually sent their children to boarding schools in one of the cities. I remained in the mission school.

For a few months, two of my fellow students were boys who had greatly enjoyed terrifying me with an enormous scorpion they had captured, huge and black, on my first day at the mission station. They had been waiting on the stone terrace, extremely pleased with themselves, on that first afternoon at the welcoming gathering. They had saved the scorpion, the most massive they had ever found, just for me.

"For you," they had said, as they put it up close to me, large pincers moving. I think it was a major contributor to my night of tears. But we were long past that.

Our teacher taught all the grades. She taught nearly all the subjects. She took over much of the teaching others had been doing to free up more of their time. We ranged from first grade to seventh. She taught on a screened-in veranda, or porch, that served as our schoolroom. We were on a solid schedule every morning, without fail.

In her one-room schoolhouse, or school porch, she sat at one end of the long wooden table that served as our communal desk. As adventure after adventure rolled over our little classroom, she maintained her happy and energetic stance toward life. And then a day came when something highly unusual occurred.

Most unexpectedly, a native of New Zealand, a former member of the Royal New Zealand Navy, strode onto our mission station. I never heard how it was, exactly, that he came to decide to visit our mission at just that time, but there he was.

Our outpost station itself had originally been founded by Christians from New Zealand, so perhaps that is why he gravitated toward what had been the New Zealand missions. He had gone to university in South Africa and then later worked in the education field, mostly in the New Zealand established mission areas in the north of Zimbabwe. But there he was... this movie-star handsome man walking onto our mission station and into all of our lives. But then... you know how this story goes... He kept coming back. And a year later, he and my teacher were married. Our very own version of a fairy-tale romance, with two most memorable characters, which easily outdid any Hollywood couple for their sheer star power.

No one in their right mind would have dared attempt to coordinate these two strangers meeting, on that remote plot of ground in the bush country of Africa—he from one continent and she from another. We couldn't even guarantee from time to time how long it would take us to travel the dirt roads or to make it through the rivers, much less plan anything so amazing. A fiction author would not have dared put it in a book; no one would have bought the storyline. But it happened.

It was a big lesson to me. That following what you perceive to be God's leading, in faith, and keeping a positive stance on life can lead to rather startling life events. I never forgot that.

But to me, she remained my teacher.

I hope, for all of us, that someone, somewhere, looks back

and says that we taught them well. Because the truth remains, we do teach the people around us, for better or worse. Day in and day out. For good or bad. Whether we want to or not. We teach them by our lives and by our actions—by our faith or the lack of it.

For me, in addition to the school knowledge, I learned the simple yet profound lesson that a girl can follow God's leading for her life and also greet each day, even out in the middle of the bush country, with a gigantic smile and a gleam in her eye.

Thank you, God, that Your work in our life is not dependent on our calculations and clever planning; it's only dependent on our following You and doing whatever it is You have led us to do, at any given moment. I thank You for that wonderful fact. Thank You that it is always easier to just let You have the reins.

15

The One Connection

———— ✺ ————

Sometimes my family took the long trip in our green Peugeot to the nearest town. I eagerly awaited this trip for one highly important reason. There was a bookstore there. It was small, with only limited books for sale, but its small size did not deter me for a moment. It contained the one thing I most wanted: the next installment in my favorite series of books. English author Enid Blyton's wonderful series, *The Famous Five*, resided on the bottom shelf toward the back of that beloved store. I saved all my allowance for this one thing, for this one trip to town, for this one store.

I excitedly hurried to the little bookstore, located on the wide main street, while my mother headed to the butcher and other local stores. I sat cross-legged on the cool floor and looked at the beautiful covers of my favorite series, pulling out the next one in the set. Relishing seeing them all there together, lined up like that. Grand stories, full of windy English moors and abandoned buildings, of mysterious caves on the wild sea, of dangerous rows across harbors in the night, and always, the packed lunches of ginger beer and cold meat sandwiches that they were ravenous for. Of perilous danger and daring rescues. *The Famous Five*. Full of mystery and clever detective work by four children and their dog. Boyish Georgina, clever Julian, shy Anne, and stout Dick. And, of course, Timmy the faithful and smart dog. I carefully took my book home on the hours-long journey, to read, re-read and add to my own bookshelf in my room. I sat beside an oil lamp at night, eating one of my mother's homemade rolls, reading my new book in the circle of light.

I don't know who decided to build and stock the one single bookstore in that town. I don't know if they had conversations about the pros and cons of income or feasibility. But I do know that life would have been much different had they not built their little bookstore. At least my life would have. The store was my one connection with the outside world of books.

We are all someone's one connection. On our mission station, we were many people's one connection to the possibility of an education or medical help. But it's just as true today, at this moment, for each of us. We are all someone's one connection to something. Their one connection to love, a kind word, a book well-written, a community theater program well-done, a roadway well-shoveled or mail well-delivered.

Supporting a child through one of today's many children's aid programs, writing letters to them, may mean you are that child's one connection to hope.

Many American Christians seem very wrapped up in finding their purpose. What they don't realize is that they already have one. Every day we are presented with an array of opportunities to have purpose—to dynamically impact every person we meet.

We undervalue ourselves, our friends and our acquaintances and utterly misconstrue our own impact in this world if we think otherwise. Every single one of us is someone's one connection to something. Solomon, the wisest man, said that *As iron sharpens iron, so one person sharpens another* (Proverbs 27:17). It's the way the world works. We affect each other.

In a highly technological world, it's easy to not believe that anymore. But it is still just as true. While I have certainly not read all the millions of websites and all the millions of Twitter messages, I *have* had my thoughts greatly informed and stirred by certain sites, blogs, and messages.

What if they hadn't bothered? What if they had thought there were so many already out there that theirs would be of no use? But you see, I can't look at all the sites out there because that would be overwhelming. I am just one person. I happened to be helped by theirs. I can't listen to every song that's ever been composed, but I have been profoundly blessed by some that I have been privileged to hear. I'm so glad those artists did not feel lost in the shuffle and give up. For they were my one connection to what I needed to hear.

I watched a young man arrange multicolored produce at the grocery store the other day, and the care and the artist's eye with which he was doing his work intrigued me. He was engrossed. That day, he was my connection to a moment of beauty, and it brought a smile to my face which no one else had managed to.

And that is the way of the world. There will always be only so many people that we know. There are only so many neighbors living on one street, only so many places to visit or live. Just as there are only so many people who will get up at the crack of dawn and plow your road. So next time the snow plows go by before the sun comes up, let's not use the word they as in glad they are out, but let's peer a bit deeper and see the human figure in the dim light of that truck cabin. It's a person. And that person is your connection to getting your road plowed.

If you've never read Enid Blyton's children's mystery books, you may need to be prepared that they will feel out of date and from a different era.

But then again, they may be just the connection you have been looking for.

God please help me to understand that I truly am the one connection that many people today will have—to a smile, a sincere word, generosity or to kindness. They may see others today, but no one else takes my place. And help me to truly see those around me for what they, too, are giving to me. Pull me out of complacent dullness and open my eyes to the people around me. They are my connections to many good things. And sometimes, they even encourage my connection to You.

16

The Builders and the Mechanics

Today, we often see people at the top of the business world making millions of dollars while those near the bottom make only a sustenance-level income and are often considered to be of less value. However, I was shown an entirely different system as a child.

Back in Tennessee, at the college my father had taught in, I witnessed first-hand the great value everyone attributed to the dairy farmer who ran the dairy that was situated right in the center of the campus. There was also high regard for those who worked with him.

On our mission station, too, our community rose and fell based on the contribution of every person.

Every single thing we had on that station was based on someone's work—every vegetable grown, every brick made, every load of firewood gathered, and every well dug.

The bricks to build the buildings on our station were made

right there using huge water and clay pits, vats, enormous sieves, large wooden racks filled with the clay mixture, and nearby kilns so hot that the air around them shimmered from the heat. The brick-makers, with sweat dripping down their faces, slowly lifted and slid the huge racks, now filled with the red clay mix, into the kiln opening. Then the bricks dried in the sun before being carefully stacked up high in preparation for the next building project. There was no moment of thinking that the buildings around us had just appeared.

We hired the brick workers from the surrounding villages, and we paid them a very good wage—enough to send their children to school and for their families to have good food. At night, they dragged thorn bushes over and positioned them around the carefully stacked up bricks. Cows had been known to come wandering through at night or early morning, knocking over the stacks of bricks.

A number of the people on our station were not only teachers or preachers, doctors and nurses. Some, in addition to these other duties, knew how to fix things. We had built a garage on the station to repair and service our vehicles. One of the missionaries, who was also a bush pilot, was in charge of overseeing that area. In addition, we hired and trained people from the surrounding villages and gave them work as mechanics in the garage, and some of the older teenagers on the mission helped out there too.

It was from watching all these efforts at keeping things running out there in the bush that I gained an admiration for the immense contribution of people who know how to repair, build and fix—an admiration that has never left me. The people who can figure out how to fix things and make things work… To run a station such as ours, they were invaluable.

Their ingenuity was startling. We had a generator on our mission station. It sat in a special place of honor, and the word *generator* was said every single day, as in, "The generator is up and working again," or "Oh no, the generator is down." The generator at our station was precious to us, as was the much smaller back-up generator residing beside it. It provided our hospital with all its electricity though the staff had learned to function at times without it.

The original contractors who had come out into the bush to help with the set-up, a few years before my family's arrival, had wired the entire compound so that, even though there was no public electricity for one hundred miles, we did have electricity to our homes during certain hours of the day from our generator. They had figured out how to siphon off enough power from the generator for those hours before the hospital needed full power again. I can still see my mother, racing to get her iron, and hurriedly ironing clothes and plugging in everything electric. But in the evening we would light our tall Aladdin oil lamps with the beautiful chimney globes, and also some lanterns to place around the house.

A journeyman plumber had laid pipes around the station from one of the deep wells that had been drilled so that we could have running water, but that was an up and down situation. Because we lived on drought-prone land, and there were many contingencies such as water pressure to deal with, we often hauled the water to the house as the pipes laid waiting for a better time.

An internal phone situation had been rigged up so we could call each other across our compound. We had no access to outside phones, but we could at least talk to each other unless our little system went down. Then someone would set about fixing it.

Thousands of schoolchildren were taught in buildings constructed from the ground up. The builders took great care to make those brick buildings as strong and sturdy as they possibly could. Thousands of sick people were treated in the hospital that the mechanically-minded kept running. Long truck trips were made to bring in supplies for our survival and upkeep. It was a constant conversation in the background of every day, these making-things-work discussions.

The generator. The bricks. The grand moments of electricity. The water wells.

And the builders and others who made things work. Some people taught classes one day and were busy working on fixing things the next. Some had been raised on farms and had a strong background in how to fix things.

Those job labels did not signify menial labor or boring functions. Oh, no. They were part of our lifeblood. They were, in fact, our very backbone. We could not function without them. We were living far too close to the land to take anyone's work for granted.

It's interesting how far adrift society floats from understanding what makes things actually work. Is the person who makes pencils for the student to write with or writes the amazing textbook less important than the teacher? Is the teacher less important than the administrator? Is the person stocking the shelves with food items less important than the person putting the food items from the shelf into their cart? What about the person who prayed for rain during the drought? And the person who sold the farmer the seed?

There seems to be an inherent need in people to contribute. In a group discussion, the light and sense of well-being that comes over someone's face when they are told that their comment was a great contribution to the conversation is proof enough. The look on a child's face when you tell them that the task they accomplished will brighten the classroom is proof. The sad look on an individual's face when they feel they have nothing to offer is also proof.

In the animal world, the level of contribution to the pack is always high and constant. It seems to be only humans who begin to tell each other that they might not be necessary, that they have nothing to offer.

Somehow we've reached the place where we make judgments on personal value instead of understanding that unless we truly value every person's contribution, we simply won't make it as a people or a society.

I think that we could all probably repeat the apostle Paul's words to ourselves every day until they are emblazoned irrevocably in our minds: *"Even so the body is not made up of one part but of many... As it is, there are many parts, but one body. The eye cannot say to the hand 'I don't need you!' And the head cannot say to the feet, "I don't need you!"* (I Corinthians 12:14, 20-21).

In my mind, I see the flurry, hear the panic, as frightened, sick people were brought into our mission hospital and our medical appliances were not working. And then the sound—that loud noise—as that huge generator kicked back on. And we all breathed a sigh of relief. The generator was working. We were back in operation!

Our missionary mechanics had done it again.

Father, please don't let me ever fall prey to the notions of a culture that has decided to pay select people exorbitant sums even though their job is in no way more important or difficult than that of the many others. Help me understand reality, not made up ideas of celebrity or status. Help me know the truth: that the people putting food on my table and keeping my electricity on are valuable in my world—valuable to me this very day. Thank You so much for their skills. Thank You for their work.

17

Answering the Call

I'm not sure how someone flies hundreds of miles in the dark in a small plane over the African bush, with no lights anywhere below, but I know of a pilot who did. He came to rescue the youngest child on our mission station, a precious little girl, in the middle of the night. He landed the plane between two lines of fires that we had built along the sides of our mission runway strip to illuminate his touchdown. And then he took off, with our little mission girl on board, to fly hundreds of miles to the largest city hospital in north Zimbabwe.

The plane disappeared into the night, its blinking lights fading high in the black sky, leaving us in the darkness with our many kerosene lanterns, the distant light of our hospital glowing faintly. And raging orange-red fires to extinguish.

We were living in a time and place where outside communication was slim. With no phones or computers, getting the word out that something was wrong had been a large undertaking.

However, we did have a shortwave radio, and though we didn't know if anyone could hear us, we pounded out the message in the darkness.

Our mission doctor had watched that night as his only child grew more and more ill, and after every resource in our hospital had failed to save her, we fell to our knees in prayer. Word of our situation was transmitted through the shortwave radio and desperately relayed forward and the minutes of sickness and high fever ticked on.

And then—the miracle in the night. Word came back to us. Someone was on the way. Many miles away, a pilot—a crop duster by trade who none of us knew—had heard our frantic message and was at that moment boarding his plane to come for us. The adults on our mission station, both missionaries and Africans, hurried out into the blackness with lanterns and flashlights to clear ground around our small runway strip and set about building large fires to outline its path. The pilot would have to set the plane down between the lines of fire.

Our little girl was saved. Many days later she finally came home, over bumpy roads, back to our mission station with her doctor father and her nurse mother. We loved her so.

I cannot forget that night. Out of sheer darkness, help arrived, and a talented man landed a plane between wide lines of fire.

The people who rise to the occasion, who do what needs to be done—they are a special breed. The ones who instinctively know they have the skill to do it, and when their turn comes up, they don't shirk. Their years of practice pay off, and they can do the unimaginable. They are my heroes.

I have many times watched people worry over what their life purpose is and where they should spend their time, wasting countless hours in the process. And they are often told the quite useful advice: "Do what you love, and God will use it."

But you know what? There's something else that is just as true. If we just keep doing our job and learning the skill or the trade in front of us—whether or not we love it—if we apply ourselves, God can also use that.

That's what a crop duster pilot did when he heard the faint, frantic cry of some missionaries deep in the bush, trying to get a message out to someone. I have no idea if he liked crop dusting. What I do know is that his many years of maneuvering in that plane, day after day, were all practice for something extraordinarily important in our lives.

Paul says, in writing to the Ephesians, *For we are God's handiwork, created in Christ Jesus to do good works, which God prepared in advance for us to do* (Ephesians 2:10).

I'm sure there are many ways, mysterious ways, in which God prepares in advance for the good works we will do. But I would guess that in addition to giving us gifts and abilities, one of the ways is simply having us show up for work. Over and over. Like a crop duster who just went to work every day. And when that work was turned over to God, a story, that is very often still told, occurred.

That pilot knew how to fly. And fly he did. On one of the most hazardous journeys I've ever heard of. Deep into the African bush he came. And he flew our girl to safety.

I wonder what it looked like to him as, far away in a dark sky he approached us that night, and in the deep darkness saw up ahead, below him, appearing out of nowhere, those lines of fire.

To this day, I am in awe.

———✒———

Lord, instead of worrying so much about what I should be doing, help me to do what is in front of me. Give me the courage to walk out in the gifts and abilities that You have so graciously placed inside me, and let me never disparage what Your Word says is also Your handiwork—myself. Thank You for creating me, thank You for making me, and I praise You for each one of us. Help us turn ourselves back over to You, the Creator, and walk out in power, freedom and truth as Your creation. In the name of Jesus, who holds everything together.

18

The Rains

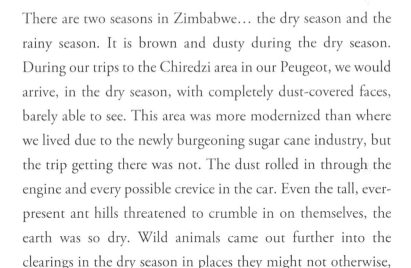

There are two seasons in Zimbabwe... the dry season and the rainy season. It is brown and dusty during the dry season. During our trips to the Chiredzi area in our Peugeot, we would arrive, in the dry season, with completely dust-covered faces, barely able to see. This area was more modernized than where we lived due to the newly burgeoning sugar cane industry, but the trip getting there was not. The dust rolled in through the engine and every possible crevice in the car. Even the tall, ever-present ant hills threatened to crumble in on themselves, the earth was so dry. Wild animals came out further into the clearings in the dry season in places they might not otherwise, looking for water at any watering hole they could find.

Until a person has experienced drought, they don't fully appreciate the rain. Though farmers around the world have a high respect for the life-supporting power of rainwater, most of us don't fully appreciate the utter necessity of those downpours until we have lived through a season of true drought. Not just dryness, but drought… when the land begins to wither under our feet, the grass turns a worrisome dying brown and trees are in root distress and start to rapidly shed their leaves—in summer, not autumn. When crops lay sad and useless in their fields.

The rainy season in Zimbabwe is an exhilarating, dramatic time of year. It descends in something of a wild crash upon the savannah. Warm days turn boiling as the heat builds up and storm clouds gather on the horizon, slowly piling thicker and thicker until they seem massive. The whole world turns a bluish-gray, and the already hot air stops moving.

There is a growing anticipation that you simply can't miss. And, eventually, a breeze arrives, filled with electricity; and with thunder reverberating, and lightning cracking on the granite slopes of Zimbabwe… the rainy season arrives. Torrents suddenly flow where for months there had been only dry ravines.

I would hurry outside; the air charged with those electrical currents and feel the first drops of water hit my skin. Then the downpour. I would stand there, letting the rain pour over me, soaking it up. Then my friends and I would run to the nearby stream, suddenly overflowing its banks and rushing at full speed, and jump in, letting the water rush past us. It felt so good. Our skin cried out for water. During the rainy season, little pools appear everywhere; streams overflow and lakes are high. Water abounds.

Everything needs water. As it says in Deuteronomy 11:11: *But the land into which you are about to cross to possess it, a land of hills and valleys, drinks water from the rain of heaven* (Deuteronomy 11:11 NASB). Drinking water from the rain of heaven. A beautiful thought.

The lavish, purple jacaranda trees in the cities bloomed splendidly just before the Rains, their soft petals falling everywhere to create pathways straight out of fairy tales. Then the Rains came, and the jacaranda gave way to the magnificent flame trees. It is a sight never to be forgotten.

But we were in the bush, where there were only a few jacaranda and flame trees, though someone had planted several in our own backyard. What we saw as the Rains came was the brown before us turning into an ocean of vivid green as the world seemingly sprang to life again. It seemed someone had taken a gigantic brush, dipped it in green and swiped it across the plains and mountains in front of us. And we and the animals, and everything around us joined as one to turn our faces to the beauty of water.

Balance is everything in life. Too much of a dry season and our hearts and crops wither. We lose our food supply. Our skin cracks, like the ground beneath us. Too much deluge and we have floods and things are destroyed. Homes are underwater, and people clamor for higher ground.

We long for and need, the one; then we long for and need the other.

Modern people often deride the old cultures for the

intensity with which they prayed for rain. Until, that is, the modern people are in drought. Perhaps some of those cultures were praying to the wrong gods for rain, but at least they were close enough to the land to acknowledge their need. But even the most modern person, when the drought persists long enough, begins to understand a basic fact of our existence: we must have water.

When the apostle Paul was preaching in Lystra, in Turkey, he made this statement: *In the generations gone by He permitted all the nations to go their own ways; and yet He did not leave Himself without witness, in that He did good and gave you rains from heaven and fruitful seasons, satisfying your hearts with food and gladness* (Acts 14:16-17 NASB).

The Rains of Africa. I can almost feel them now.

God, thank You for the witness to Yourself that You have given in all Your creation. Thank You for the rains. I pray today for rain for all the places that so need it. We thank You for this gift. Let us not be so taken with ourselves as to not acknowledge its source: You. And please bring our planet into balance again. Protect us, as the old prayers say, from drought and floods.

19

Crocodiles

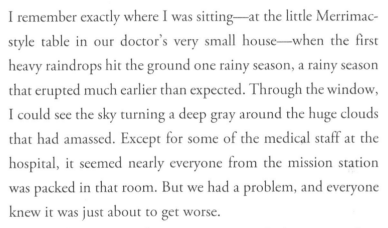

I remember exactly where I was sitting—at the little Merrimac-style table in our doctor's very small house—when the first heavy raindrops hit the ground one rainy season, a rainy season that erupted much earlier than expected. Through the window, I could see the sky turning a deep gray around the huge clouds that had amassed. Except for some of the medical staff at the hospital, it seemed nearly everyone from the mission station was packed in that room. But we had a problem, and everyone knew it was just about to get worse.

Five of the women from our station, including my mother, and a couple of the nurses, had gone into town in our old Peugeot the day before to get some supplies. The plan had been for them to gather what they needed and make the long trip back the next day. The rains had seemed a number of days off still. We had been sure the women would beat them, based on our experience of watching the clouds. However, we were wrong, and the drops of rain currently hitting the window by my side at that little table proved it. Every minute now counted.

I watched as two Land Rovers pulled up outside the house. People hurriedly put on hats, and rain gear and equipment were stuffed into the back. Containers of gasoline were loaded in. We always carried our own gasoline with us wherever we went for refueling purposes, as there were no fueling stations for long miles. When the government of Rhodesia declared its independence from Great Britain, sanctions were imposed and gasoline was rationed, crippling our travel and making it even more complicated for us to have enough to get around.

"We have to go meet them at the Turgwe," had been the verdict reached less than half an hour before, in the doctor's little living room, as the first drops hit. "They will never get across."

We knew what was coming. The torrential downpour clearly on its way would flood every river in the vicinity, and my mother and the others would be stranded. The men wanted to get to the large Turgwe River first and set up what they needed to guide, push or pull the car across the river. It was very important that the women not attempt that crossing without something on the car with the river so high. More than one mission car had floated off down river.

The men were so focused on the task at hand that they said yes without much thought to us children riding in the back of the Land Rovers along with the equipment. So of course we piled in.

The rain grew stronger as we drove, and the Turgwe was flooding by the time we arrived. We climbed out of the Land Rovers, and the men began immediately preparing in anticipation of the Peugeot arriving on the other side.

Our Land Rovers had a winch, a steel cable, attached to a roller motor on the front. Someone could wade or swim through a river and attach the hook at the end of the cable to a strong tree, then start the roller motor and pull the Land Rover through the water to the tree. In this case the men were going to attach the cable to the Peugeot and pull it toward the Land Rover on the bank. No one was paying much attention to the children. It's not like we were really going anywhere, and we were a group of seven, so we certainly weren't going to get lost.

We were already wet and relishing the sense of the water after so much dryness. The river looked deeply inviting. We dove in and swam or waded out to the middle. It was sheer exhilaration.

We had been told a hundred times not to get in the rivers or any standing water. We knew we were doing the wrong thing to enter that water. I, myself, had been given an hour long, personal lecture on the scientific dangers of parasites by our mission doctor after he returned from a tiring day at the hospital late one afternoon. After finding me playing in standing water near the place where we made our bricks for the station, my parents had already done what they could think of to straighten me out. Hence, the hour long doctor's discussion was supposedly another effort to pound sense into my risky thinking.

The Peugeot soon drove up. And stopped on the other side of the bank. The men were waving at them from our side. But the women jumped out of the car, all at once and in a frenzy.

"Get those kids out of the water!"

It seemed like they all yelled it at once. The men turned and looked at us, seemingly in unison, as though seeing us for the first time. They were all concerned, and rightly so, that the water carried bilharzia parasites, for which there was no medication at that time. Or that it carried one of the many parasites that caused river blindness or a host of other diseases. But the river also carried another, more immediate and worse danger. One they hadn't known about.

While we were unashamedly laughing off their concerns yet knowing at some point we would indeed be forced out of the water and in trouble yet again, my foot slipped. Then it slipped again, into a long, yet shallow, highly defined groove. And then another one.

My friend beside me, a very bush-savvy young boy, turned to me, a suddenly strange look in his eyes.

"This river is filled with crocodiles."

I stared at him and knew he was telling the truth. He, too, had just slipped in their grooves. His sharp eyes were scanning the river, the bank, everywhere. And he knew. He knew what was lurking in the dark reaches of the water, underneath and unseen.

"We have to get out. Now!"

The refreshing rain falling on the river, the glint of the rushing water, the fun of swimming—none of it mattered from that moment on. What mattered was the fact, the *fact*, that in the murky darkness of the bottom of the riverbed—right where I was standing—silent, lethal killers were waiting. Waiting for just the right moment. With every intent to kill.

Crocodiles.

The walk back through the rushing river was very different from the excited, fun-filled walk out. No more eager splashing in the water, laughter, or seeing if we could find where the water was chin deep from the mix of falling rain and the gushes of water running down grooves on the bank slopes. I had gotten far out into the river, in the very middle, and it was swelling by the moment. Gingerly, in fear every time my foot landed on the bottom and slid downward, I made my way back to the bank. In fear. And now in truth. Back through the river as it really was. A bilharzia parasite-infested place full of crocodiles.

I will never forget that walk back.

Temptation is like that. It looks all glorious at the beginning. Only occasionally does it present its true face. Instead, we are caught up in its lies. The person who is not our spouse seems so understanding and sees the real us as we want to be thought of… until, strangely, we begin to have trouble with them, too. The drug really does help us study… at first. The alcohol actually does make the room seem brighter and our conversation wittier... until we can't think like we used to. The stolen money does buy the clothes and jewelry that people compliment us for... until the day they see our name is in the paper for theft.

Temptation's wages are brutal. Destroyed families, children who no longer can respect their father or mother, financial ruin, smeared reputations, loss of self-esteem. Just like the devouring crocodiles, which kill on one strike

The Bible says that when we are faced with temptation, God will provide a way of escape (I Corinthians 10:13). For me, that escape boils down to one phrase that I always remember: "Get out of the river." Sometimes the thing that has gotten me into the most trouble is when I know I am being tempted, I know I am toying with a wrong path, and yet I keep on toying, when the best possible thing to do is to simply get out of the river, to completely remove myself from the sources of temptation, just as fast as I can.

It can be a long, slow walk back. Sometimes we get so far out into the joyous river of our temptation that it is a terrifying walk back to the bank. Because, in our effort to get back to shore, we are still in the river. Going in the right direction now, perhaps, but still working to get ourselves back out of the water.

"This river is filled with crocodiles."

That statement takes me back. To the horrendous feeling of knowing crocodiles could be swirling around, in the water, coming up from behind, at any minute. Hungry. Desirous of bringing me down to a watery death.

Because crocodiles eat people. And so can temptations when we do not run.

Father, help me to always get out of the rivers of my temptations. Help me to know quickly when there are crocodiles in the river of temptation, no matter how invigorating and enjoyable the river might look. Give me the strength to always turn back around, no matter how far out I've gone, and make my way safely back to shore. Please keep me safe.

20

Water

―――――∽―――――

Africa is a place of beautiful waters. Of powerful rivers—the bending Niger, the long Nile, the glittering Zambezi, the vastly deep Congo River, and the alternately placid and raging Orange River. It is a place of magnificent waterfalls—the Blue Nile Falls, the Kabwelume Falls, the Ngonye Falls and, of course, Victoria Falls. The continent of Africa is a place of gorgeous lakes, such as Lake Nakuru, Lake Kariba, Lake Tanganyika, Lake Victoria, Lake Tana and Lake Kivu.

And Africa is a place of barren lands and drought. Of deeply encroaching desert. In huge swaths of land, people walk for miles on end just to carry enough water for one day. A place where people are dying from lack of clean water.

A significant part of the time that we were in Zimbabwe was during a season of difficult drought, and water became quite scarce. The two boreholes on our mission station were going dry and had to be shut down except for a couple of hours a day so that the pump would not burn itself out trying to pump when there was no water. Boreholes were dug by boring straight into the ground with a large, drill-like piece of equipment, then inserting a long rod or pipe that reached the underground water and aquifers. Nearly all of the water that the pumps on the borehole did bring up during the drought went immediately to the hospital. I would sit in the back of our truck, on top of barrels and containers, ready to ride with our driver down to the borehole and fill the containers up with water to deliver to the rest of the mission.

Later on, churches in America sent money to build a reservoir for the mission so that there would be a back-up plan for water during drought, and the principal of the secondary school took on the oversight of that huge project. I learned early the meaning and the value of water. It was not a given in my life. There were days when I had one inch of water to try to take a bath in. And that is fortunate compared to what others, both then and now, suffer from regarding lack of water.

I love water—I love fountains, waterfalls, rushing rivers, oceans, beautiful blue lakes, hot springs and even little birdbaths in the yard. Standing under a waterfall, putting my hands under a fountain or dangling my bare feet in a mountain stream is great joy.

Water is the stuff of life. When we send out long range space capsules to collect specimens or take pictures of faraway planets and stars, whatever else we may be looking for, we are always searching for one significant thing—possible clues to even the microscopic presence of water, the basic need for life as we understand it.

Our bodies are comprised mostly of water. Our blue planet has a high percentage of its surface covered in water, much of it salt water. Beyond all doubt, water is one of the core resources of our earth. Without it we do not survive.

Whatever the reasons, there seems to be little doubt that climates around the world are somehow changing in our time. Whether these changes are from man-made problems or just the earth's normal cycles, time is growing shorter in terms of finding ways to deal with them. People who once had plenty of water are going to need to be taught how to cope with drought.

Some people think that in days to come, water will be traded on international stock exchanges, it will be worth more than some gems, and it will be hoarded and sold. I hope these are only alarmists, and that they are wrong.

I do know that the Sahara is moving south at a somewhat startling rate, sweeping more and more land into its abyss. And that the people, where I live, are becoming more and more concerned about the chemicals and pollutants finding their way into what were once pristine water supplies.

To grasp what is happening to our world water supply is a somber and thought-provoking experience. The statistics on children's deaths worldwide from drinking unsafe water are staggering.

I have lived in places where every drop of water for human

consumption had to be boiled. Always. Where many bodies of water contained dangerous parasites. It is not a simple matter to find clean water when surrounded with these conditions.

There may still be time for us to change our ways, to help those who need help, and to help ourselves. The world at large does have the resources and technology to address this situation, at least in some ways.

We must ask two questions.

First, how do we live with ourselves knowing that there are millions of little children around the world today, many of them in Africa, struggling mightily for a simple drink of water? And even millions more struggling for a drink of *clean* water. I have often wondered how I am going to discuss this subject— my own efforts, or lack thereof—with my God when I stand before Him face to face. What words will I use?

And the second question: If we allow the pollution of our local water supplies to continue, wherever we live, where will all of us end up?

Jesus said, *Let the little children come to me...* (Matthew 19:14). How will we bring the little children to Jesus if we haven't managed to get them enough water to even stay alive?

Jesus said that whether we respond to the hunger of those who are hungry, and the thirst of those who are thirsty will determine how he views us. In fact, he says it is how he will judge us.

I was thirsty and you gave me nothing to drink... Then they will answer, "Lord when did we see you hungry or thirsty?"... He will reply, "Truly I tell you, whatever you did not do for one of the least of these, you did not do for me" (Matthew 25:42-45).

Many people have high-minded ideas of what God will ask us about on Judgment Day. They seem to think he will ask us theological or even political questions. Personally, I'm concerned that he's going to ask us about the water, since he said he would… because I'm honestly not sure how I will respond.

How will you answer that question?

———&———

Father, I pray that I will be a conduit to the children of this world for both the living water of Jesus and the earth water of your creation that keeps us physically alive. Please show me where best to put my efforts, money and time in this regard. Bring to light those people who are getting the job done and empower me to support them. I thank You so much for their efforts. Please, please help these thirsting children. Help me to not stop crying until the job is done.

21

A Price

———————— ∽ ————————

It was a boiling hot, dry day when I opened the door to our little tin house and heard the sound of sobbing. Not just any sobbing. Heart-wrenching, gut-wrenching sobbing and gasping. It was my mother. She was flung across the bed; the pillow already soaked from her tears. Her own beloved mother, my grandmother, had died. We had just gotten the word. I threw myself down beside her, also in tears, as much for her tragic pain as anything else. I don't know when I have felt sorrier for anyone.

My mother's family meant the world to her. There was no money for a ticket back to America. Her sisters, brother, and her huge extended family would gather. And she would be here, in a hot, dry place—far away and uncomforted. I thought she was going to die there on that bed, crying until there was nothing left of her.

These days, people and organizations put up money for

individuals to go back and forth from the mission field or on short mission trips to help out in so many assorted places, and it's so wonderful. But there just weren't those options then. Few people had the money or means to do that.

My mother's family sent her pictures of the funeral, one with my two older brothers, who were representing our family, standing beside the headstone. I don't know how many times I have seen that picture. My mom looked at it over and over. She missed her boys. She missed her mother. She missed her sisters and brother.

My father's mother also died. We had moved up the hill to the bigger house by then, and he sat in his chair by the window, staring in pain. His book and glasses had slipped unnoticed onto the chair. He, too, would not be going home for that.

Then my second oldest brother Jim got married. I would not attend that wedding, which mattered a great deal to me. My mother found me sitting on the floor in front of the fireplace, sobbing, clinging to his picture that we kept on our mantel. My brothers were both much older, and Jim had stayed in America for college. I missed my brother.

And I held the water-stained, faded yellow, typewritten telegram, many days late in arriving, letting us know my second little niece had been born. My oldest brother Ron's second girl. "Mother and baby both fine. We love you very much." Such good news but heartbreaking for us to not be there.

The list went on. Some things were small, others large and significant. The road my parents had chosen in going to Africa carried a price.

Those things cost us. No, they were not the worst that could ever have happened. The members of my immediate family were all alive, on both sides of the ocean. But the road carried a price.

Because every road has a price.

Even the right roads, the best ones, the ones we are certain of both before and after we take them. Every road carries the price of what would have happened on a different road. Not that we ever could truly know that other road. It seems so unfortunate that we have created a society where people are taught that if there is any price to pay—any lack, any hardship to endure—then things must have gone wrong. Even our best and right choices preclude other things.

The good that came from my years in Africa is incalculable to me. But it doesn't mean that there wasn't a price. The sooner we stop the madness of thinking that if we can't have it all then things must have gone terribly wrong, the better we will be. There are people all around who spend hours upon hours lamenting roads that were not taken many years ago. It's a folly that destroys the present.

I know of many people who have chosen highly meaningful professions that meant they would not get big paychecks. My oldest brother decided to become a pastor while in the middle of training to be an engineer, a profession with a much higher pay. I think he made the right decision. But both roads had their own unique price attached.

There are roads taken, and roads that are not.

If we have missed our best guidance from God and have found ourselves on an unwise road, God will pick up with us at any point and begin to powerfully use the road we are on if we ask Him. And, if we are fortunate enough to have found ourselves on a good road that came about by strong guidance but nevertheless involves a price, God will also make certain to use that road as well.

You make known to me the path of life, says the psalmist (Psalm 16:11).

A price, like my mother's precious, painful tears, does not mean that the road was wrong.

Because He never wastes our roads. Never. No matter what. Only we can do that, by not turning those roads over to Him.

———⌒———

God, please put and keep me on the right road for my life. And when I'm off of that, please work with me anyway. I need You to help me put one foot in front of the other, especially when I don't know what I'm doing. Make use of everything. And help me find Your best for me. And show me how to encourage others, to find the path You have for them.

22

Doing Good Works

I have watched people go into mental contortions trying to decide where they should put their energy, and I admit I have been guilty of this myself a few times. Mostly an exercise in self-focus, it probably has another, worse name. But on we go, trying to decide where to volunteer, where to spend precious time, where it will benefit the most—sometimes, I hate to say, instead of actually getting to the *doing* part at all.

It is at those times that my mind drifts back to my mother, and the world comes back into clarity. Quickly, easily, and without unnecessary stress. The answer, she showed me, is most often what is right in front of you.

My mother was a doer of good works. The reason for this was that she engaged the needs right in front of her, without thought of the gain to herself or any pretense at all of the grand importance of those good works. She didn't put her picture in fliers or give speeches about the importance of what she did.

She just did what came to her. I can see still her, back in America, at garage sales, looking for shoes for the children of an alcoholic man who was spending his money on drink—she had noticed his children were nearly barefoot. She just took it upon herself, quietly, to set about finding shoes for all the children and dropping them off when she stopped in for coffee again with the harried wife. It was an effort filled with dignity. I don't think the children ever knew. I remember coming home and seeing all those shoes lined up and asking her what in the world was going on.

Once she heard of a pastor in northern India whose children needed clothes, and she wrote to find out the sizes and went around buying them new clothes and mailed them off. She took countless meals to people who needed them. She stayed up numerous nights with friends. Most of her good works were not publicized or even known. But they were great. And partly accounted for the numbers of people who never forgot her, even in old age.

The hospital on our mission station was a popular place for women from surrounding villages to come to give birth to their babies. It had become clear to numbers of people that there was great value in giving birth there; the medical staff was loving and skilled, and the mortality rate was low.

Many of these women, leaving the hospital with their one-or-two-week old babies, only had old, rough or torn blankets to wrap the infants in and little in the way of clothing, socks, little slippers or caps. One of the first nurses to arrive at our mission had set about writing letters back to America requesting help in the way of good clean clothing for these infants.

My mother took over this responsibility as a help to the medical staff... and also because she adored babies. She was a firm believer that every baby deserved to start life with a good solid, soft blanket and nice clean clothing. Not just one piece. At least a few. And diapers. Real cloth, good diapers. That was very important to her in this project.

The hospital staff had set aside a small room just for the effort, and it was packed from floor to ceiling with infant clothes, all in sweet little colors and soft fabrics. Tiny socks, small white T-shirts, everything imaginable for those dear little souls. And many hundreds of colorful soft blankets. I wish I had any words at all to explain the pride and joy on those new mothers' faces as they dressed their little ones in the soft clothes and wrapped the brand new blankets around them. There were often tears.

My mother spent so many hours in that little room. Organizing what came in, and then bundling it into individual little layettes, the blankets wrapped nicely around all the other clothes and gifts. We have a picture of her in that room, surrounded by all the rows and stacks of beautiful clothes. Her face simply beamed as she worked.

As far as I know, she didn't wrestle one bit with whether or not to take on this project. It felt quite simple somehow. And that's how it always was with her, no wrestling around with concepts or feasibility studies. She just did things in front of her, and that worked.

I somehow think that probably does work the best. I can think of a number of fairly large helping organizations that were started by someone with just that same view. They saw a need and started putting things together to meet it. Piece by piece. Then it grew. And others joined in. And that's how it always was with my mother too. Some of her endeavors remained quite small, or were just one-time efforts, like the shoes for the alcoholic man's family. Done quietly on the side, with no fanfare at all. Others were larger and gained a good bit of notice. But I'm not sure she saw any difference between them.

So I think this may be the right way to decide where to place our energies. Perhaps we could just look around and ask ourselves: "What is in front of me?" And then go do it. And if that is over quickly, just move on to the next thing. And if it's not over, maybe stick with it. Or turn it over to someone else.

Good works don't have to be complicated.

At least they weren't for my mother. Her good works were woven through our lives, like the thousands of threads in a well-made garment. We often didn't notice those threads, but they made it strong and held everything together.

It's unfortunate that today the idea of simply doing good works is sometimes compared to legalism, or, when it comes to Christianity, seen as a means of earning salvation. But that's not true. Good works are those wonderful things that affect each and every one of us, such as when another individual does something that helps, changes or encourages us. A good work makes a powerful difference. They are *called* good because they *are* good.

For we are God's handiwork, created in Christ Jesus to do good works, which God prepared in advance for us to do (Ephesians 2:10).

A truly fascinating thought—that we are actually created to do good works. Works prepared just for us to do. It's sobering, exciting and inspiring. And the next good work to do is likely right in front of us.

Right in front of you. And right in front of me.

God, please show me the works You have prepared for me to do. Since they are most likely right in front of me, I also pray that You will open my eyes to see them. Don't let me worry so much about doing the grand things as about doing the things I see at this moment, the ones I actually can do. The ones I may be tripping over. Thank you for letting me have some part in spreading goodness in this world.

23

Victoria

The Smoke that Thunders

The Zambezi River is one of the greatest and most beautiful rivers in the world. From the mountains of central Africa, the Zambezi flows through six countries, a glittering blue jewel that makes its way to the Indian Ocean but not before it unexpectedly plunges downward, over 100 meters, to create a wild and breathtaking sight—Victoria Falls.

Given that name by the Scottish explorer, David Livingstone, this most extraordinary plunge of water was originally named Mosi-oa-Tunya, "Smoke That Thunders," and is one of the most astounding sheets of falling water in the world. During the rainy season, the water crashes over at stupendous speed, and the spray alone is an exhilarating sight to see and feel. Rainbows are everywhere, even in the moonlight. It is one of the Seven Natural Wonders of the World and has been named a World Heritage site.

I have always found it hard to explain what Victoria Falls means to me. The power of the water alone is riveting, the sound overwhelming. In terms of sheer area, it is the largest falling curtain of water on earth.

And the Zambezi—river of legend, movies and adventure, the river of Africa's history.

One night, I found myself suddenly awake in the little cabin I was staying in on the Zambezi River. The night was incandescent from the glow of a full moon. I sat up and gently pulled back the flimsy white curtain that covered the window above me and looked out at what would have been an eerily silent world were it not for the entrancing sound of the ever-moving waters of the Zambezi, flowing by in the night. In the center of my view, right in front of the moon, at the edge of the river, stood an enormous buck, still and unmoving. It was the most beautiful thing I had ever seen.

It was on the shores of the Zambezi that I was chased by baboons, and where I found myself unexpectedly standing right in the center of a large herd of hippos, alone and completely surrounded. I had been following their footprints and came right up on them. Perhaps my favorite place on the Zambezi was an island filled with thousands of monkeys. They were everywhere, swinging from trees and running on the ground. It became almost overwhelming. Clearly, the island was theirs, not ours.

Much has changed now around the Zambezi River and

Victoria Falls. Now there are many more tourist attractions. I am glad I saw it when I did. I suppose many people feel this as they get older and watch "progress" overtake more rustic, wilder times. But then, I didn't see Victoria Falls as David Livingstone first saw it, in all of its wild glory. And he didn't see it as it must have been a century before that. Time moves on, as it always does.

"Scenes so lovely must have been gazed upon by angels in flight," were the words of David Livingstone in 1855, regarding the majesty of Victoria Falls.

I, too, find myself thinking of angels when I think of Victoria, and I'm not sure why. But he was right to say what he did. Maybe it's just the sheer power, the sheer realization of something so uncontainable.

Places so far away can be momentarily reached by the divine messengers, the angels. And all places can be seen by God. The entire world is seen by our Creator, which makes me think of the times those angelic beings suddenly showed up, seemingly out of the blue. Suddenly there with Jacob, as he slept. Suddenly there in the fiery furnace. Suddenly in the prison where Peter was chained between guards, breaking the chains off of him and walking him out. Suddenly talking with Abraham while on their way to destroy the wicked Sodom. Suddenly appearing to Daniel the prophet by the river in all their burnished bronze brilliance.

We can pray for someone across the globe, God's power goes forth and their lives are touched. It can be instantaneous.

There is something about standing beside Victoria Falls that I think might make even a hardened person realize that there is power in this universe far beyond us humans.

Victoria Falls is one of the most gripping marvels I have ever witnessed. And for me now, it stands as a reminder of the power of the One who made it. One who has power far beyond anything else that exists anywhere.

One for whom nothing is impossible. With God all things are possible (Matthew 19:26).

David Livingstone was right. Angels most likely did gaze upon Victoria, long before our ancestors were ever born.

As Moses said, some 3,000 years ago: Before the mountains were born or you brought forth the whole world, from everlasting to everlasting you are God (Psalm 90:2).

There are some things that are powerful in this world. The Smoke that Thunders is one of them. And then there is something far more powerful than that.

The one who made the Smoke that Thunders.

God, don't let me pretend that You are a controllable thing or idea that we can make up to suit ourselves or mold to what any current fashion might enjoy. You are Your own. Your power is beyond me. Beyond us. Beyond all we can ascertain. We are still just trying to figure out the world You made. Give us the humility to understand, as so many of the ancient peoples have known, that there is indeed a great Creator. One, above it all.

24

The Animals of Africa

———————— ✑ ————————

Nothing could have prepared me for the exhilaration of standing on a windswept plain and seeing Cape buffalo by the thousands, from where I stood all the way to the horizon. Or for excitedly counting 200 wild elephants in one day. For the sight of lions, viewing me at dusk from the tall golden grass, almost hidden, their keen eyes always watching. For giraffe gracefully swaying in the crimson sunset while zebra wandered below them.

Nothing could have prepared me for an island with thousands of monkeys swinging from the trees. For the terror of being chased by a group of baboons and barely making it inside as they crashed against the door, scratching and scraping at the screen as it slammed shut behind me or being chased by a charging bull elephant, trumpet raised and ears flapping. So many times I watched as herds of beautiful impala leapt gracefully in front of us as we yet again stopped the Land

Rover, car or truck and waited patiently for them to cross the dirt road as we made our way to or from our mission station.

The list of animals was so long—the painted wild dogs, vervet monkeys, rhinos, cheetahs, waterbucks, gorgeous sables, wildebeest, elands, kudus, and on and on. They were magnificent, sentient creations of God.

Once when we were staying in a rustic cabin on a small hill, far out on the savannah, the lanterns were extinguished, and we sat for a long time in the darkness just listening to the various, eerie sounds below us—a movement, a strange howl, a rush and then the cough of a leopard. The call of a lion. Then quiet and yet more movements in the night. There is nothing quite like the sound of Africa's wild animals moving, unseen, in the dark.

And nothing, then or now, could have possibly prepared me for the unbelievable abuses that are wreaked upon these animals of Africa. As much as there are those who care about their lives and preserve their right to exist, there are others who willingly mow them down in merciless pain, hacking off their tusks and body parts and leaving them to die—poaching them to make ivory trinkets or potions for vendors both in Africa and numerous other places. It is bloody, cruel, tormenting and evil. The fact that this is allowed to go on without a world uprising is a travesty that will lie at the feet of the human race. Some predict that elephants will disappear from their native habitats within the next two decades if the madness is not stopped. The mountain gorilla, white rhino and cheetah are also in a state of imminent danger.

Why have so many humans descended into a state of such degradation that they have no concept of the value of life? And equally important, why have so many people of faith forgotten that the same Creator who made them also spent enormous time and energy creating the other life forms on this planet?

We sat around the dinner table late one night in the light of our oil lamps, finished plates pushed to the side and listened intently to a young man just up from South Africa. He told us of his new job tranquilizing wild animals to be transported by truck and then shipped to America for trophy hunters to "hunt" in enclosed preserves. The animals would arrive, completely out of their natural environment, stripped from their family units and weakened from shipment. And for no reason except for sport—not even for food. It was disturbing beyond measure as we sat by the dim circles of light after dinner, listening to stories of this terrible market just opening up.

As I contemplate the carnage that is ravaged upon these creatures, both in the past and the present, and the heroic efforts of the people who are attempting to save them, my mind turns to my own country.

Many say it was Chief Seattle of the Duwamish Native Americans of North America who said, "How man treats the animals today is how man will be treated tomorrow."

The implications of his statement are profound. Is the disregard for the value of animal life one of the signposts we should have noticed on the road to our disregard for human life?

At the very least, we should not condone the merciless killing of a life to simply make ivory knickknacks or so-called potions. And not turn a blind eye to much of the useless and cruel testing performed on animals by cosmetic companies, universities and other industries until they are through with them—their bodies destroyed and wracked with pain.

I respect Albert Schweitzer, the medical missionary to central West Africa and winner of the Nobel Peace Prize, deeply. I was living in Africa the year he died. He said, "Until he extends his circle of compassion to include all living things, man will not himself find peace."

Whenever the taking of a life is done for fun, and killing is perpetrated only for enjoyment, then something has changed— on a profound level. It is at that moment that humans take themselves out of the reality of the necessity that the rest of the animal kingdom lives in.

Albert Schweitzer also said, so well, "Anyone who has accustomed himself to regard the life of any living creature as worthless is in danger of arriving also at the idea of worthless human lives."

Perhaps we owe it to our Creator to rethink our presumptuousness and our callousness.

God said to Noah, *I now establish my covenant with you and with your descendants after you and with every living creature that was with you—the birds, the livestock and all the wild animals, all those that came out of the ark with you—every living creature on earth* (Genesis 9:9-10).

If covenant talk between God Himself and the animals doesn't make us think, then I am not sure what will.

We are not quite as great as we try to convince ourselves. We, too, are created beings. Or, perhaps we *were* created with greatness in us, and we were told to be caretakers of the animals and the earth around us, and this is how sickeningly far we have fallen from that task.

I, too, enjoy posters of cute animals. But saving them from unspeakable torture is more meaningful.

And, perhaps a few dollars to those valiant people trying desperately to protect them would be in order.

———❦———

The prayer of Albert Schweitzer:
Heavenly Father, protect and bless all things that have breath: guard them from all harm and evil and let them sleep in peace tonight.

25

Languages

———————— ⌇ ————————

Language is universal. Astronomers say that even the faraway quasars, the most distant and brightest spaces in the universe, are sending out electromagnetic signals.

Language, in all of its thousands of various forms, is communication.

The heavens declare the glory of God... day after day they pour forth speech... (Psalm 19:1). Once again, the language of the Bible embodies sound scientific principle. It's too bad we ever relegated it to fanciful allegory.

In addition to the heavens, the entire earth also reverberates and resonates with the sounds of communication.

Elephants communicate with each other often, and many of the sounds they make are too low for the human ear to hear. They can communicate with lost family members, many miles away, who are greeted with great emotion when found. They can also, startlingly, differentiate between human languages.

Renowned for their long and accurate memory, elephants use many gestures and sounds every day to communicate on an assortment of subjects and can remember individual people and their actions toward the elephant community for decades. Crows, extraordinarily intelligent creatures, also have an enormous range of vocalization. Due to its complexity, research efforts to understand the breadth of the language of crows have been slow. Communication between dolphins is also extensive and complex. Researchers believe that dolphins communicate emotional states as well as factual information to each other.

Communication drives our lives on a staggering array of levels. Even our cells and nerves send signals to one another. It's how we think. Whether talking with ourselves on an internal level through our thought life or with our fellow humans by audible words, we are driven to communicate.

From the Latin word *commūnicāre*, meaning *to share*, we constantly share information. Intelligence professionals watch for the tiniest cues of hand and face movements to communicate to them whether someone is telling the truth or not. We also communicate volumes of information to others, whether intentionally or unintentionally, by how we spend our money and how we use our time. We immediately communicate to others how we view them by how we treat them.

The apostle Paul said that angels have a language. *If I speak in the tongues of men or of angels*, he wrote, *but have not love, I am only a resounding gong* (I Corinthians 13:1). Again, this part of the Bible is also so often dismissed as poetry, but I think Paul knew what he was talking about. Angels can communicate with one another and with us.

My first interest in a language other than my own was sparked only days after arriving in Zimbabwe. I was told that when I was communicating in Shona, the answer to the morning greeting of "Good morning, how are you?" was "I am fine if you are fine." Or, "I slept well if you slept well."

Later, that simple greeting became symbolic to me of the tribal and community orientation of the people. Words change us. They shape who we become. It would greatly impact one's concept of the world to greet friends each day with a word of community, "I am fine if you are fine," instead of "I'm fine, thanks."

Every language on earth carries in it a seed—a piece of knowledge that the other languages do not express as succinctly or as completely. Think of the many descriptions for snow found in the Inuit and other Native Eskimo languages. Or the words used in ancient Greek to describe the various kinds of human love.

Language also carries reflections of culture. There are words in Chinese with no real English equivalent, only long phrases of explanatory meaning that even then nearly miss the mark. Individuals who communicate only in sign language are often adamant that those who can hear cannot fully understand their language. It takes nearly a paragraph of explanation in English to approximate the translation of a loved and commonly used Dutch word having to do with warm togetherness and friendliness. Some German words are hard to translate to their full meaning in any language. English, a difficult language to learn by many standards, is filled with idioms that are used almost without awareness by native English speakers.

Each language seems to carry some nuance, some understanding, that the others do not. So many times, I have had the meaning of a word from another language explained to me over and over before the light finally came on. Each time it was exhilarating to realize an entire concept could be encapsulated by one single word, even if not a word from my language. It was as though I had been searching for that word, somehow, all along. All languages seem a part of some greater whole, some greater understanding that we find ourselves yearning for.

I had a friend in Zimbabwe, a charming and lively young African girl. She had such a great smile. She spoke only a smattering of English, and I spoke extremely little Shona at that juncture. But we were so drawn to one another. We sat together on a rock ledge, pointing and laughing—talking, or at least it seemed so at the time. As we would wander about holding hands, we were also communicating, even if we realistically couldn't have done much talking, at least not in the same language.

Communication has more to do with desire and feeling than with words alone.

The two of us sat high up on the side of a hill one hot day, watching the proceedings of a baptism in the river below as my father waded out into the waters and people gathered on the river bank. The late afternoon African sun was glancing off the blue waters of the river.

We weren't paying the best of attention, too busy communicating—laughing, looking into each other's eyes and seeing what the other thought about what we were pointing and laughing at. The memory brings a tear to my eye, of joy, but also of wistfulness. The language barrier is real. One has to want to get across it. One has to put in the time and the work to fully cross it.

Much later, when I was in Ghana, there were so many languages, dialects and sub-dialects. At the other end of the road we lived on, people spoke a different tribal language. It made it difficult for us at first though my father immediately set about learning the two major languages in our area so he could communicate.

Sometimes I have a similar feeling today, in my own culture, to the feelings I had on that street long ago in Ghana. Yes, there are a number of different languages being spoken around me, but that's not it. I'm referring to the fact that even when I'm among people who are speaking my own native tongue, it's as though we are still speaking different languages.

But we are not. We are simply talking at cross-purposes. Meaning something different, though we use the very same words.

I long for clarity. I long for straight-forwardness. For honest speech. Or maybe… maybe it has more to do with the *listening*—with the heart connections. With honoring others for what they are trying to get across without pouncing on them. Like my little friend and I.

You have to want to hear.

And you have to want to understand.

———&———

God, let me listen in the way You would have me to. Let me listen as Your creation speaks and praises You, even though I do not always know what it is saying. Let me listen as Your people try to communicate. Let me listen with my heart. And let me listen to You. To Your word, to Your Holy Spirit, to You. Show me how, Father; show me how to listen.

26

Diamonds

———— ∽ ————

There is nothing wrong with diamonds. In fact, there is much right with them. Riveting elements of astounding beauty, they come up to us from deep within the earth. Few things equal the raw shining glory of these stones. One of the hardest substances on earth, a diamond can cut through surfaces nothing else will touch.

God instructed Moses that the breastplate of judgment for the high priest was to include a diamond. *You shall make a breastpiece of judgment, the work of a skillful workman... You shall mount on it four rows of stones... the second row a turquoise, a sapphire, and a diamond* (Exodus 28:15,18 NASB).

In fact, the city of God itself is covered in pearl, gold and jewels of many kinds. (Revelation 21:19,21).

As with most things, diamonds were created good.

But, as we have done with so many things that have no inherent evil, we have managed to corrupt almost the word itself with our own greed and abuse.

At age ten, during a family trip, I stood above the huge Big Hole of the Kimberley diamond mines in South Africa, probably the largest hole ever dug into the earth by hand. Further north was the mine where the Great Star of Africa, cut from the Cullinan diamond, had been found. I knew what the Star of Africa was—it was, at that time, the largest cut diamond in the world, and I had seen it.

When in England, we had gone into the padded, silent and darkened room in the Tower of London and seen the breathtaking Crown Jewels of the United Kingdom. And there, mounted in the King's Scepter, on instruction of Edward VII, was the multifaceted, breathtakingly beautiful Star of Africa. And in the Imperial State Crown sat the Lesser Star of Africa, also cut from the Cullinan Diamond. The diamonds were majestic stones of a master creator, cut by master craftsmen.

And unearthed on the backs of slaves.

The history of South Africa is inextricably linked to the diamond mines, and much of its glittering wealth was built upon them. It is very likely that the basis of what later became modern South Africa as we know it began in the diamond mines, and that the apartheid that would finally come to full birth in the 1940s was first conceived many years before in those same mines. Though the colonialists in South Africa had adopted an early form of 'pass law' in 1815, saying that black Africans could not move about freely in white owned areas without a pass, it had been quickly revoked, in part by the loud voices of the anti-slavery movement that was gaining momentum in England.

But, in 1872, black Africans were denied any right to hold land in diamond mining areas, and the Pass Law was reinstated, this time denying Africans the right to wander about freely on their own lands as well as the right to leave the job they had been given, for any reason. Though skirting the word slavery due to new, strong sentiments against it in both America and England, the burgeoning diamond owners of South Africa managed to install it anyway—they just renamed it, and the stage was set.

It was the Prime Minister of South Africa, the famous Cecil Rhodes, founder of the most famous diamond mining company in the world, who articulated in the late 1880s what would later become the travesty that finally birthed in South Africa. He advocated for class legislation, for Pass Laws, calling for the indigenous natives to be treated differently than the white race, who would rule over them.

He managed to initially silence the British missionaries who spoke out loudly against his policies, though others of the missionaries agreed with him, and at least one even aided him. It was Cecil Rhodes and his emissaries who cruelly tricked the Matabeleland Chief, Lobengula, into signing away rights to much of the gold, and also the land, of the country Rhodes eventually named after himself—Rhodesia. Missionaries of the time arrived at Lobengula's compound, too late, and he asked them to examine the papers he had signed for Rhodes. In dismay and anger, they translated and read the fine print to him.

We were touring the old diamond mine during a journey down to Cape Town in South Africa to visit a family there. I found the country to be remarkably different from Zimbabwe. Everything felt different, even the air itself. I have heard others make this same distinction, and though I've tried, I can't explain it.

Things were definitely not right in Rhodesia; the effects of colonialism, the racism and the usurping of land terribly damaged the people there. It had been a grievous sin, brutal and cruel in its implementation. In some cases, the African people had been forcibly removed from their homes and ancestral lands, murdered or beaten, and their villages burned to the ground. Their enormous herds of cattle had been stolen or cruelly slaughtered. The people had been herded into wagons and relocated to dry, arid land to endure ongoing poverty.

But the particular brand of apartheid in South Africa was something different yet again. It was in full swing when we were there, and it was utterly disturbing. Nelson Mandela had been recently locked away in prison, with by far most of the years he would spend there still ahead of him. The white cities seemed highly modern and westernized for the time and the black townships a massive disgrace.

I had a European friend from Zimbabwe whose sister in Johannesburg had to quickly hide her servant's baby under the bed so that the infant would not be found when someone unexpectedly knocked on the door. The baby, who did not have the necessary papers to be in the city, thankfully gave no cry from its hiding place. I remember thinking at that moment that this was the worst place I had ever heard of.

We drove up the beautiful coast near Port Elizabeth. I fell in love with the sterling blue Indian Ocean. We saw the fun surfers at Durban. We visited the just burgeoning upscale areas of Cape Town. But I recall feeling so confused by everything, and just wanting to go home, back to Zimbabwe. No, not just to Zimbabwe, I wanted to go back to the people living in the Tribal Trust Lands. They should not have been forced to live there, but I preferred being there with them. I didn't want anything to do with this place.

Even though I know great and even successful effort has been made for change in South Africa during the long years since, and I am now friends with wonderful people from various backgrounds there, it has been hard for me to let go of those initial experiences.

Sometimes, when I look at the twinkling stars, sparkling like brilliant diamonds on a dark surface, or I look at the diamond in my mother's wedding ring, I simply ask—why?"

Why do people have to ruin the best things? Why do they degenerate into despicable actions and into greed and hatred? Why does the word *diamond* now have to carry with it these thoughts of slavery and hideous actions? Why can't we live right?

Maybe it's too much to expect the world at large to even want to follow pathways of justice, integrity, and fairness, though I would certainly like to think that people, in general, could rise to those attributes. And, sadly some professing Christians only hold the form of godliness and do not actually live by its power and truths, as it says in the book of 2 Timothy 3:5.

But it's not too much to expect from those of us who say we truly believe our God. And not too much for people of character anywhere who want to create a better world.

As Micah 6:8 says: *And what does the Lord require of you? To act justly and to love mercy, and to walk humbly with your God.*

That Scripture and its meaning was sorely missing in the diamond mines of old South Africa.

Father, forgive us. Forgive us for travesty. Forgive us for not honoring the beauty of Your earth. Forgive us for the mishandling of Your gifts from the earth, and for the mistreatment of our fellow human beings. Dear God, show us all a better way, a truer way. A finer way. Show us the way of honor. Let our lives reflect Your love, Your light and Your graciousness as a diamond reflects the light. Please help us all be part of setting things right. Of redemption.

27

Under the Trees

———————— ✑ ————————

Many of the churches in the villages and areas surrounding the mission station met under trees. The Bible College students all had the well-maintained bicycles that we had purchased with mission money, and they rode out for hours on end sometimes to reach these churches and preach. Some of the churches under the trees had long wood-hewn benches, lined up in rows that were carried off for other uses during the week. Or the benches just stayed under the trees for other types of meetings or activities. In other locations, there were no benches, and church members sat on the ground. In a few places, a school had been built so we met there.

On hot days, the trees provided shade and protection from the heat. Sometimes a breeze wandered through. Those services under the trees were some of the most beautiful I have ever attended.

Some of the services under the trees were held under the

ancient baobab trees. The baobab, in many ways a symbol of the African savannah, is an enormous tree that grows to a great height and has the ability to store water in its huge trunk. People and animals have actually lived, protected, in the huge hollow trunks of older baobab trees. Its fruit has a flavor similar to lemon, and its flowers are beautiful. But it is mostly recognizable for its shocking enormity and its upside-down look, as though the roots were on top during the dry season.

Other services were under an acacia tree, where we could see the weaverbirds, with their fascinatingly woven nests dangling from limbs. Whether we were under a baobab or acacia tree, it always had the sense that we were in a delineated place, not just out in the woods trying to experience nature, as is sometimes done at camps and such. We were there because that is where the church met.

It wasn't always optimal. There were the seasonal rains, of course, and then it was hard to meet. But I find I get mildly frustrated at hearing people refer to meeting under the trees for church as somehow primitive. I loved it. Meanwhile, there is certainly nothing wrong with getting a roof over our heads. It's a natural inclination of the human race. Just as birds build their nests and bears go in the caves; as the lions find good, well-shielded areas, and the elephants set off on their journeys to more suitable living arrangements—so humans have always, it seems, set up thatch, wood, cement or bricks to keep the elements out and keep themselves safe.

Our own mission station had a large meeting room in one

of the schools that served as our mission church, where many came each Sunday. We had rousing worship, good teaching and heartfelt prayer in that room. The Zimbabwean people sang simply beautifully. It's like a natural gift. Perfectly gorgeous harmony seemed to just appear, like some inherent cultural trait, and those Shona songs were melodious to listen to. Sometimes I feel that I can almost still hear the echoes of the singing. I find myself singing them even now though I can no longer recall what every word means. Music is like that. It stays with you.

But there is something special about worshiping God under the trees, with their swaying branches, as so many have, or a large steadiness as the baobab tree has. Trees give shelter and provide habitat for so many animals and even other plants. They give a sense of stability to the world, I think. They tend to live a very long time—many for hundreds or even thousands of years. It seems comforting to sit under them, knowing that. And to speak to our Creator with them nearby.

The prophet Isaiah said, *My house will be called a house of prayer for all nations* (Isaiah 56:7). Jesus quoted that Hebrew Scripture when he cleaned out the temple from those attempting to profit off the people.

I don't think it matters where we meet. I think God accepts the worship of the nations in whatever form their buildings take. Or in no building. As Jesus said to the woman of Samaria, *A time is coming and has now come when the true worshipers will worship the Father in the Spirit and in truth, for they are the kind of worshipers the Father seeks* (John 4:23).

And as the martyr Stephen said, *The Most High does not live in houses made by human hands* (Acts 7:48).

It was simpler under the trees. But, yes, I know... I don't live there anymore. It was a time, for the most part, that is slipping away. But it was simpler, ever so much more straight-forward. It felt clearer to me then somehow.

And, at least it seems to me anyway, the same number of people came to know Jesus. Come to think of it, I think maybe more if it is a headcount we're looking for.

Even today, I love to sit under a tree and read God's word and pray. God speaks through nature, and it speaks of Him too. And, He sends His love to us through it.

Father, help me to honor whatever You are doing, wherever You are doing it. Move me past any predispositions I may have in regards to appearances, any preconceived ideas. Let me watch for Your Spirit, for Your actions, and make decisions based only on that. Bless my fellow believers, wherever they might be meeting today.

28

River Washing

———————— ⌂ ————————

There were a few ways out of our mission station, and all involved fording more than one river. One road led through a river that was notorious for problems, especially in the rainy season… Thankfully, we did not need to go that way quite as often. The other main dirt road also led through two or three rivers, including the largest in our area—the Turgwe.

Many women of the surrounding villages went to the Turgwe, to wash their family's clothing. They chose the wide Turgwe because it was swift; the water came coursing down rapidly over the rocks, yet they could still maintain footing, and if an article of clothing got caught in the water, it was retrievable with a quick response. The women scattered through the rocky, cold river water, beating on their clothes to clean them and then dousing them in the running water. When a piece was finished, it was carefully laid out on a higher rock or across low tree branches, to be bleached dry in the hot sun.

Clothes washed this way are clean. It may seem surprising now, with our plethora of washers, machines, level guides and detergent choices. But it's amazing what clear running water, beating on a rock with soap and bleaching them in the sun can accomplish. A little rough on the clothes, perhaps, but it worked.

Cleanliness matters. Not as a definition of value, but in an operational sense. It gets harder and harder for us to operate when dirt and grime set in.

Have you ever tried to make an important decision with things out of control around you? Sitting in your kitchen with unwashed dishes piled up, with laundry overflowing the hampers and the floors grimy and unmopped? It's hard to think. Your mind feels disordered and cluttered. It's easy at those times to make a reactionary decision, not a proactive one. Imagine sitting in the same room with glistening curtains, clean floors, bright counters, and a cup of coffee. You can focus. You can think. You can hear.

And how does all this work spiritually? When we are rid of the sins that bind, our understanding is different, our listening suddenly unencumbered. We don't get as easily misled. Our decisions are more centered.

As David, the psalmist, said, *Have mercy on me, O God… wash away all my iniquity and cleanse me from my sin…* (Psalm 51:1-2).

The cleaned up state of our lives does not in any way determine God's love and watch-care over us. It very well may, though, determine the clarity with which we can hear. It might help or hinder our ability to go further in with God.

Create in me a clean heart, O God, and renew a steadfast spirit within me (Psalm 51:10, NASB). I have learned how it feels when I am aware of God's work in cleaning up my heart and when my spirit seems right. But what does it *look* like?

For me? It looks like startlingly white clothes, clean as can be, drying on rocks under an African sun as hot as blazes and next to a brilliantly cold running river. They'd been through a lot to get clean, those clothes. But I'd wear them in a minute. They were beautiful. Truly beautiful.

And truly clean.

Father, I pray for the desire to allow You to clean my life as You see fit. To make me a vessel that is usable and durable. I pray that I will always gravitate toward Your will and that I will not falter as my life is shaped to do Your work. I pray that my spirit will be one of joy and not of sorrow, that I will embrace Your work in my life as You make me a sparkling and steadfast child of Yours.

29

Frangipani and Mahogany

———— ∽ ————

On our mission station in Zimbabwe, I had a bedroom that would rival some I've seen in glossy magazines. The other day, at the local bookstore, I saw magazine pictures of glamorous men and women carefully posed in front of a quite simple but exotic villa bedroom that charged thousands of dollars a night, and the thought crossed my mind …

I had a bedroom like that once.

Strange, isn't it? But I did. It was not fancy; it was a simple, rustic room with wide window screens framed with wooden panels, and outside of it stood the rich beauty of Africa. It was surrounded on one side by mahogany trees and on the other by frangipani trees. And that was just the beginning.

Behind the curtain of gorgeous trees was a large swath of land that contained so many beautiful, outstanding flowers. A riot of flame lilies grew near my windows. Behind the many subtropical flowers stood one of the huge granite outcroppings, or *kopjes* as the Dutch named them. A path wound its curving way past my windows and through the trees to meander on down the hill. I was older when I realized that people take expensive vacations to go to exotic places like the path outside my bedroom window.

The house itself had a pleasant stone fireplace, and verandas encircled almost the entire structure to let the breeze in from every angle. The view from the front step rivaled probably any in the world: the massive African savannah surrounded by a semicircle of hills dotted with villages and in the center an open vista where one could see the faraway, misty blue and purple mountains that formed the border with Mozambique.

Thinking about it all got me to wondering.

What is exotic, anyway? Is it the glistening snow on an old city lamppost in Chicago? Or is it green corn growing for miles on end, waving gently in the breeze? Maybe it's a lush New England pathway and covered bridge. Perhaps it's gigantic ocean waves crashing in on a cove, reminding us of pirates and hidden treasure, or the golden sun, setting over the desert.

Perhaps our angst is that it is we, ourselves, who have somehow grown jaded or tiresome, not our beautiful planet. Perhaps it is we who are in need of reawakening to the magnificence around us this very moment.

People travel all around searching for a beautiful spot of nature. They find it, are filled up briefly and then slowly dissolve again into what they term a mundane existence. These are the eternal vacationers, searching for something to fill a lonely place inside. I wonder if that remains the difference between the vacationers and those who have a love of nature deep in their hearts—those who love nature see its beauty everywhere, in the rock by the road, in the bird overhead, in the tall grass by the creek.

The book of Ecclesiastes says, *He has made everything beautiful in its time* (Ecclesiastes 3:11).

I like that.

The gorgeous mahogany trees outside my bedroom produced a beautiful hardwood, much in demand. I had many of the glossy black pod seeds with their bright red tops just laying around my room as decoration. I thought they were pretty. I could lie on my bed or open the doors to my own little private veranda off the bedroom and allow the wondrous, fragrant aroma of the flowering frangipanis to drift in, carried by the breeze. The lovely frangipani flowers started off as a cream color, changing to a deep yellow before they dropped off the tree, which was also a beautiful sight as they lay across the ground. It was a splendid, peaceful way to fall asleep.

But, there was also the fact that each morning, in that bedroom, I had to tap my shoes on the bedrail before putting them on—to make sure no scorpions, especially the baby ones, had crawled inside during the night. They seemed to like to do that, getting right down into the toe of the shoe, and it was common practice to tap shoes before putting them on, to route the scorpions out.

And, of course, this was the bedroom that had been the

target of the python we had encountered on our very first day, the one that was shot off the face of the earth by the kind missionary lady we were staying with.

And, as well, the house where the green mamba liked to sun itself of an afternoon.

But it was exotic, as per current definitions.

So is my cast iron birdbath out in the yard—exotic, I mean. I was just refastening the bolts the other day so it wouldn't tip over, and I refilled it with fresh water as I do each and every day. The water sparkled in the morning sun as it splashed in. Suddenly a flaming red cardinal darted by, watching for the new water.

That, too, is exotic.

Father, don't let my views and understanding of beauty be limited. Of people or of places. Let me see the real beauty. Open my eyes, like the eyes of an artist, to see the hues of color as they play across Your world. To see the single red flower in the path of gray stones. Open my eyes. To see the beauty in an old woman's face, when she smiles her charming smile and her eyes light up when I come in the room.

30

Days of Peace

They say we never know what we have until it's gone. Sort of a hopeless statement, I've always thought, and I would like to think that surely we can do better than that.

The apostle Paul said, *I have learned to be content whatever the circumstances* (Philippians 4:11). It's a tall order. And part of making it work is to force ourselves to look for the good when things aren't perfect. To stop focusing on what is wrong and start focusing on what is right, even if at first we have to really search for it.

To find that place of peace in ourselves, and then string the days together with it.

What is peace? Peace is a good conversation with one's sister or brother, completely free of shades of rivalry. It's walking home in the brisk morning air from a polling place on Election Day, knowing that no matter the outcome, you have voted in line with your conscience. It's accepting on a gut level that you cannot control the world, and that the only control you have is over yourself.

Peace is standing over the grave of your parent, knowing for certain that all is forgiven between you, in both directions. It's standing there knowing that there is deep and abiding love present on both sides of that grave.

A strange, sobering peace, that one.

There is no way to put a price tag on days of peace. When they're gone, we long for them, with a longing that is nearly inconsolable.

When trouble strikes, all we want in all the world is to go back to just one of the days when the ordinary marched on and nothing was wrong. We would give all of our wealth to be rid of the trouble and go back to the days of peace.

So why is it that we so struggle to appreciate them when they are here? I think it may be because we have learned to put such a premium, such a laser-like focus, on any little single thing that may not be perfect. Not quite up to our standard. We allow the bits of negative on a perfectly normal day to overpower the cornucopia of goodness that might be trying to flow our way. I have discovered that petty discontentment is a destroyer of a high order.

I can think back to so many things in Zimbabwe, little things, that brought such enjoyment. First comes the memory of Kariba Bream, surely one of the most marvelous tasting seafoods anywhere. Fresh and delicious. Oh, to have one now. Next, watching some members of our hospital staff grill flying ants to perfection out in the back of the hospital, for a snack. Not for the patients, just for them! They grilled them as often as they could. I thought it unbelievable that they were eating the ants though they insisted it was a delicacy.

I crouched by the cast iron grill pan with them, watching as the ants sizzled over the fire, shaking my head. Although I did not care to eat one, I have heard of things that are far worse, in my mind at least, being served at fancy New York restaurants. We had also once had a plague of flying ants on our mission station, and the memory of lying under blankets that were pulled tight from head to toe, with the large flying ants pounding away at me was too fresh in my mind to have any possible desire to eat one.

I did love sadza though, the staple of the diet at that time. It was a cooked, thickened cornmeal dish, served with greens, vegetables, or a peanut mixture, or even with meat stew relish when available.

Memories flood back of watching women in the nearby villages weave beautiful baskets in an assortment of shapes and sizes. I never once grew tired of watching them work at this exquisite craft, and they let me try my own hand at it too— and I quickly learned it does indeed take practice. Their skill was handed down from ancient knowledge. I remember the unique smell of those vines and grasses that had been soaked in preparation for basket-making. Some baskets were made specifically for winnowing grain, others for carrying or storing things. Every single one was beautiful and strong.

We had many Zimbabweans in our home for tea and for dinner, and for late night games. Many nights I played dominos by lantern light with a young friend, an African girl, in our living room. We both liked the game. I played another game with my African friends in the afternoon after school was over. We drew squares in the dirt and sat around it with beans and rocks and such, moving them around. They generally won.

I can hear the sound of the old wringer washing machine located near the back screen door as clothes were quickly put through it. I remember climbing trees day after day—one of my favorite things to do—climbing just as precariously high as I possibly could.

I recall serving our Bible College students the most wonderful evening dinner we could afford in our home to honor their graduation. I was the waitress for the event, at the long wooden table in our dining room, bringing in and clearing dishes as they sat at the table with the most scrumptious food we could manage.

The hours I sat on a rock in the hot sun by a river bank, waiting for a flooded carburetor to dry out after we had ended up floating the car through a river, didn't seem like a waste of time. We just sat and talked there on the river bank before continuing our trip. The Shona people that I lived among were experts at waiting. For them, it seemed that time was not something that gets lost or gets found, as though we are in control of it. It just moved on.

I remember walking along eating sugar cane when we

traveled to the sugar cane fields some hours away. It was a wonderful thing to eat, full of vitamins and minerals, before it was processed into molasses, then raw sugar, and finally white sugar. Some of the roads in that area were sprayed with molasses and water to tamp down the dirt, and they glistened in the sun.

My years in Africa were a time of great adventure, interspersed with so many days of equanimity and peace. Things had a slower pace. The days seemed ever so much longer. People of my parents' generation talked of this often regarding their own past—about the slower pace of life, the lack of self-imposed stresses. And I experienced that—in Africa long ago.

I long to sit in my tree again, with my book and my little stash of freshly picked guavas, with not a care in the world except wondering when the truck filled with water barrels would drive up the dirt incline. But I cannot. Even were I to go to the very spot today, it could never be the same. Things are built up; the simplicity of the era is gone—the time itself is gone. It has now escaped me.

But the feeling has not. And, I find, I have many things today that are just as wonderful, just as fine, just as perfect. One only has to look for them.

To string the days together on a strand of peace.

Today, I sit on my porch near the tomato plants I just planted yesterday, with my coffee, in the lawn chair I found on sale. The plants are growing already! At least that's what I have been excitedly telling people all day today; it certainly looks like it to my hopeful eye. I like being near them while I write, enjoying my coffee.

Days of Peace.

------◇------

Father, let me never underestimate or undervalue peace. It has a sound, a music all its own. And in the end, though its song is more subtle and less flamboyant than the many others that have played in my life, I think it's possible I will look back and love it best. So give me the grace and the understanding to appreciate it today. Give us peace—let it wash around us, our children, our friends and our times. Give us Days of Peace.

31

A Light in the Darkness

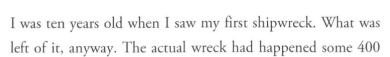

I was ten years old when I saw my first shipwreck. What was left of it, anyway. The actual wreck had happened some 400 years earlier.

My father and I walked on the white beach of Mozambique that hot, sultry morning on the coast of East Africa—a place of astonishing natural beauty, a place that can take your breath away. The glowing azure sea ran right up to pristine white sands that stretched for miles. Further down, near the dunes with their feathery green growth, lions roamed and would come right down to the sea in the evening.

In the midst of this beauty, tied down with massive and rusted iron chains, with links the size of a man's waist, was the old ship. Along with the old lighthouse, still in use above it, the ship was the one sightseeing item the entire region seemed to claim as noteworthy to visit. Little did they know that for those unaccustomed—of which there were few of us then—the very air and dramatic beauty were much more enticing.

In its day, the ship had been a Portuguese seafaring vessel. Nearby residents talked vaguely of a treasure it had carried, their story a remnant of some nearly-forgotten tale handed down to them. History books speak of ships failing often on that blue coast of Mozambique, one with priceless treasure from ancient China in it. Old stories, the facts lost now in the cold depths of a cold sea.

I stood under the steaming African sun as it cast shimmering heat waves over the ocean and stared at the old thing. Whatever it had been, and whoever had been on it, things had gone badly. Very badly indeed, for them. And here we were, so many long years later, staring at what had been their disaster, their story untold and unknown, dying a long slow death by ocean, sand and heat.

Shipwreck.

I recently read that one of the largest treasure troves ever found had been discovered in a 17th-century shipwreck in the Atlantic, where countless ships went down. It was filled with bountiful treasure sent to buy the loyalty of the Italian Duke of Savoy. It never made it. I don't know how this 17th-century story with the Duke eventually turned out, but the treasure to buy his agreement is currently being retrieved from the bottom of the sea.

How many of us, with our lives—our "ships" filled with treasure of a different kind—wreck our boats on the shoals and the jagged rocks of life?

The great lighthouses that speckle this planet, that rise high above the ground on so many shores, were put in place in a time when *light*, not computers or radar but light, was the best and safest thing to be guided by. The sun, the moon, the stars, and the lighthouses. A seaman, far out to sea, saw that lighthouse beacon, and then he knew where it was safe, where it was not and how to maneuver in the darkness he was forced to make his way through.

We live in a world that appears, in certain ways, to also be heading toward shipwreck. Oh, that the church and its people would shine out again—shine out to a world nearing shipwreck.

"This way, this way! Go this way and not over there, where the rocks will destroy you and tear you to shreds! Pay attention to the light—we care for your safety!"

For the safety of your soul.

We have heard the old stories, of pirates and scoundrels, who grabbed hold of the lighthouse and turned the great light off and misled the sailors. Or walked the reefs with lanterns to deceive the sailors and lure them to rocky and dangerous land. I wonder… how many of us have allowed scoundrels and less than well-intentioned folks to mislead our churches, our families or our children?

There were few things more serious to the seafaring communities, in those long-ago years, than the lighthouse staying in safe, rightful hands. Otherwise, disaster would strike, thieves would make off with the goods, and good and decent people would be shipwrecked.

It's of great importance to us, too, that the lighthouse of the church stays in hands that will look out for the best for the people; will shine the light of truth and valor, and will not be ashamed for the light to knife through the darkness like a penetrating signal of hope.

When I remember that wild coast of Mozambique, with its ever-important lighthouse, I am convicted of the importance of light in the darkness.

There are people at sea. Drifting.

As Jesus said: *No one lights a lamp and hides it in a clay jar or puts it under a bed. Instead, they put it on a stand, so that those who come in can see the light* (Luke 8:16).

Father, let my light so shine before people that they are drawn to You. Teach me never to be ashamed of who You are and of what You have done for me. Give me a courageous heart. Save me from treachery, from misguided thinking, whether my own or from others. Let Your word be a light to my feet and bring me safely home.

32

Matobo Hills

(Matopos)

There are places in this world where you feel you are unexpectedly in touch with an ancient past.

Matobo Hills, in Zimbabwe, is one of those places. The first chief of the Ndebele nation in Zimbabwe, who was himself the son of a Zulu chief, is buried in a cave at Matobo. The hills were given their name by the Ndebele people, and the land was sacred to them. It was called Matopos when I lived there and is now Matobo again.

"World's View," the British called it.

I can understand why. Standing on the summit of one of those granite hills, looking out to forever, one has a sense of expanse that is hard to fathom. The only other time I felt such an expanse was once when driving under the Big Sky of Texas. I had to stop and readjust my eyes. The horizon was further off than seemed possible, like the world just wouldn't end.

Scientists say the hills of Matobo were formed over 2,000 million years ago—which means a long time ago, however long it really was. They surmise that some unknown force pushed the granite to the surface to create the enormous, smooth surfaces that form Matobo Hills, so high up. "Bald Heads," the Chief of the Ndebele called those high surfaces. It is quite a climb up to them. Massive boulders are strewn everywhere, like lonely sentinels to something long past, to some upheaval long ago that we can only wonder about.

There are old rock drawings in the caves at Matobo. Old, well-done, colorful drawings that are among the most ancient on earth. There are over 4,000 in Matobo Hills alone, and many more scattered throughout Zimbabwe; many in the beautiful northeast Highlands. It makes one pause, and wonder ...

About the ancient history of the land, a history we do not know.

Something about the Matobo Hills goes back further in time than we can imagine. One can feel it, standing on those windswept rocks. Certainly much further than Cecil Rhodes and the damage he wrought, and further back than the Ndebele. Long before the ruins of the Kingdom of Butua at Khami or the ruins of Ziwa, and before the ancestors of the Shona built the Great Zimbabwe. Long before all of that, this land we now call Zimbabwe was inhabited by an ancient people in an ancient time. Some archaeologists date their findings at Matobo Hills, including tools, by thousands upon thousands of years.

Matobo Hills is where I saw my first white rhino. He was across a small flowing stream from me and was very wild. The two of us stood eye to eye, speculating about one another, about what we thought of this encounter. I could have reached out my hand to touch him. Part of me wanted to back hurriedly away; he was an imposing creature. White rhinos are pictured over and over on the ancient cave drawings at Matobo. Leopards, antelope and other animals and birds abound through the Matobo Hills, including the world's largest concentration of black eagles.

Matobo. The place where Cecil Rhodes also wanted to be buried, and, indeed, is buried. Strange. Very wrong somehow, that fact. And yet in some way understandable, at least to Rhodes.

The remains of the colonial patrol that died in pursuit of Chief Lobengula, when he was running for his life, are also buried there. How unusual. So many things, so many burial places, so much clashing history. Yet something about all of it makes a bizarre sense—like the land won't let go of the facts of what happened.

Matobo has a strange gravitational pull. It could be, as scientists have now established, that the granite shield of Zimbabwe puts off an electromagnetic force, literally attracting energy, like lightning, which strikes in Zimbabwe more than almost anywhere on earth. The granite shield exudes gamma rays, which carry the most intense energy wave of the entire electromagnetic spectrum.

The Bible says that from the foundations of the earth—through all those years of the ancient hills of Matobo, when people of the Stone Age, the Iron Age, and the various nations of the San peoples, were drawing so artistically on rocks many thousands of years ago—that God has sat above the orb, the sphere, of the earth.

Do you not know? the prophet Isaiah asked, as recorded in the Hebrew Scriptures, *Have you not heard? Has it not been told you from the beginning? Have you not understood since the earth was founded? He sits enthroned above the circle of the earth* (Isaiah 40:21-22).

I want God's blessing to reign over Zimbabwe.

There is something special in that land, in all of Zimbabwe—something indefinable. We have only glimmers, from archaeology and oral tradition, only fragments of its ancient story—much is still shrouded in the foggy mists of history.

We do not know what Matobo was called in those ancient times, long before all of these events of our own generations. We don't know who might have named it, or how they viewed this singular place with its gravitational pull.

There are mysteries on this earth, in many places, that have so far defied our understanding. Matobo, with its intense waves of electromagnetic energy, is one such place.

But my prayer is that peace will begin to emanate from the very particles of the land itself, as an unstoppable force, like those electromagnetic waves. And begin to saturate the nation. And all the people of Zimbabwe will be surrounded by the peace they have long sought, and deserve.

———— ∽ ————

God, Your Word said that You view the earth's sphere. You see us. All of us. I pray for this planet, our home. Will You help us? Help us to be part of the healing, part of the beauty, and not part of the damage? Bless the earth of Zimbabwe and let it be a place where the ancestors of the people are proud, proud of the beauty and goodness their descendants can create. Help us all create goodness in our own lands, in the places we are each responsible for.

33

Change

—⟡—

We left Zimbabwe, still called Rhodesia, during the first glimmerings of the unrest that would, years later, result in revolution and war and would ultimately devastate the nation as the African people reclaimed their homeland and afterward had to deal with corruption. But that's not why we left. My father had been asked to serve as the president of a fledgling Bible College in Accra, Ghana.

The government of Ghana was intent on making the country a place of excellence in the modern world, and that was especially important to them in the area of education. Rather astonishingly, the Minister of Education had agreed to allow our little mission to pursue the possibility of becoming one of their college institutions.

All educational institutions in Ghana at that time had to meet strict qualifications and pass yearly government inspection, so there was a rush to get the curriculum and instructors up to par so that all our credentials could pass the strict licensing criteria. The missionary family already in Ghana was very active in finding a campus, lodging for students—both male and female—and food provision and all other necessities to pass the licensing, as well as highly qualified teachers.

My father, in addition to serving as president, was called upon to teach the Greek language and other subjects, and we recruited another missionary family from eastern Zimbabwe to come as well. The Minister of Education was pleased with all that he saw, and he and his government colleagues voted to approve our plans. It was the first time the government had approved for missionaries to build an institution of higher learning, and the new college was issued an official license of operation.

Having once been unsure about going to the bush country of Zimbabwe, I now found that I did not want to leave it. I loved the bush country. But leave it we did. For many long years we continued to receive letters and calls from our African friends in Zimbabwe, letting us know, as best they could, the situation that ensued as the land was eventually given over to bloodshed.

It was heartbreaking to read and hear, as person after person was frightened, unsure, and some killed. My little friend with whom I had sat so happily watching the river baptisms wrote me years later to say that she, her new husband and child had fled from the native reserve lands to a city hoping for safety, but that she was unbelievably frightened and asked that I pray.

Our move to West Africa was hot and troubled; we had left a number of things behind in Zimbabwe for other missionaries in case they needed them, and we now seemed to not have all that we needed. Living in a large city was a first for me. I had never lived in crowded conditions, with so many people, and we had no car. It was quite some time before we could afford one.

We had landed at Ghana International Airport late morning, with me missing my home of Zimbabwe already. We were met by the only other missionary family in Ghana from our organization. My father had recruited them to come to Ghana after his pioneer fact-finding trip years before when we were still in America, and they were the ones who had done the initial groundwork to set up both the mission and the college. They had lived in the northern rainforest area and were now in Accra. They had done an outstanding job and gained much respect from the Ghanaian government by the time we arrived.

On that first hot afternoon in Accra, I sat quietly holding my satchel and listening to the adults talk. It occurred to me that I could go into the nearby bathroom and brush my teeth, which seemed hopeful, but as I started, someone rushed in to tell me to stop. Apparently, we were going to have to boil all our water, every drop—even what came out of the tap—due to parasites and a less than desirable sanitation system. I went back and sat down. We were off to a troubled start.

While Ghana has changed tremendously since those long ago days and great modernization has occurred, I think that any place that is new takes adjusting to, no matter what. Experiencing that one fact myself, over and over, has led me to great empathy for international students and other individuals today coming to live in my own country.

That afternoon there were discussions of the crime rate, which explained the heavy metal grids around windows and the yards with tall fences—some with glass on top—that I had seen as we drove from the airport. This was all different. This was not our mission station, surrounded by the people we were experiencing life with, and who cared for us and we for them. This was the big city.

Just as it had been on that day when I first set foot in Zimbabwe, there was more to come in Ghana—the rainforest of the north and the colorful, packed market full of vendors.

And my beautiful Polish piano teacher. She spoke barely a word of English and was the daughter of a Polish government official at the Polish Embassy. All the books she brought for me to practice from were in Polish. But whatever I succeeded or failed to learn regarding the piano, I learned a tremendous lot just watching this exquisite young woman who had a pure self-esteem such as I've seldom witnessed.

Then there were the nights falling asleep listening to the sounds of the highlife music from the somewhat questionable night business right next door to my window. And there was my French tutor, a wonderful African friend our family loved, but whose English was sketchy at times. I was once reduced to tears in my attempt to navigate the two or three languages he and I were attempting to communicate in.

I often stood looking out to the ocean and watching the lines of men haul in, by brute strength alone, the massive fishing nets strewn far out across the glistening blue-grey sea. I stood next to them, watching with interest as they examined the catch. I loved having a fresh coconut the minute it came down from the tree in the hands of a young boy who had shimmied up to get it. And, most of all, there were the truly extraordinary Ghanaians who we met and worked with.

Ghana. For me, synonymous with change.

It was from my mother that I learned that when change comes, when it hits you in the face, you'd better go ahead and rise to the occasion, pivot and deal with it, or it will overtake you with emotion like a ravaging bandit. Standing still is not one of the options we are given in life, as long as we are breathing and moving. We go forward with the flow of life, taking the good we can with us, or we retreat into ongoing regret.

Learn to greet the new people, figure out a way to make the new house work, even if it's not as nice, figure out a way to make the kids suddenly like bunk beds instead of having their own room or whatever it is one is facing. Because the alternative is to turn to the past and get lost wandering there. Because the present is where we live.

And our present, then, was Ghana.

Some of our strongest memories and enlightenment can come from a place we never meant to be.

Father, let me never seek change for change's sake or because I'm filled with malcontent. But help me learn to embrace real change, the necessary changes, that come my way. And show me how to help others who are also going through change. Whether exciting change or heartbreaking change—show me how to encourage, help and listen to them. Don't let me ever leave someone alone in change if I can help it.

34

Sickness

I was eleven years old when we moved from Zimbabwe to West Africa, and the first thing that happened to me was that I contracted one of the dreaded diseases—malaria. Although I had been given quinine for years, I had been in West Africa for only three weeks before it got me. We had no house of our own yet, so I lay in bed upstairs, on the second floor of the house the Wycliffe translators had rented to house their staff, and which they kindly allowed us to use while we found our bearings.

The house had a yard that was magnificent. There was a beautiful rock garden with a small pool and sparkling, tumbling waterfalls. Tropical fish swam in the pool, and flowering vines climbed the walls. A long, twisting outdoor staircase started in the garden and made its way to the second floor, where we were staying. All around the waterfalls and gorgeous gardens grew mango, avocado, pear and orange trees and banana plants. I really have never seen anything quite like it, before or since. Its one significant drawback was that it was also appealing to poisonous green mambas.

For all this fascinating outdoor drama, the house itself was quite plain inside except for one beautiful marble floor in the main room. Fairly often, the water faucets simply wouldn't work and there was no water. And no one seemed able to fix the problem.

I have no memory of the days after I succumbed to malaria; I was delirious, feverish, and tossing violently, my mother says. My first memory came as I awoke one morning at long last, the bed fever-soaked, and felt the hot West African sun in my eyes and heard voices through the nearby window from the yard below.

My mother came in, relief written all over her face to see me awake and in sound mind. For the first time in days, I could actually see her face and feel the concern in the room around me. Our new city was situated five degrees off the equator, and though the fever had finally left my body, the heat around me went on unabated. Air conditioners and such things were a luxury, from a time not yet come for us.

Difficult as it was, my brush with serious illness is mild compared to what many around the world today are facing. We live in a time of much sickness. In Western countries, there appears to be an epidemic of cancer and heart disease. AIDS and other autoimmune diseases are ravaging the continent of Africa. And as any mental health professional would attest, many people are facing depression and deep emotional distress.

My mother loved to read the poems of Helen Steiner Rice. I was much older than eleven before I had that appreciation, but there is a line from one of Mrs. Steiner Rice's poems that deeply affects me:

Where can we find the hand that will dry the tears that the heart is crying?

How can we be the hand that reaches out to those around us who are struggling with so many difficult illnesses and situations, of whatever kind?

There is so much that can be done to help people. Spending time with them, watching their children, giving them rides to various places. The knowledge that we are not alone, that we are cared for and loved, makes all the difference.

We have to simply reach out our hands, let go of judgment and just help.

Malaria, it turns out, stays in the bloodstream for about 40 years. I certainly did not know that, so long ago, lying in my feverishly hot state in the house of the Wycliffe Translators. There's nothing you can do about it. I have not been able to donate blood for most of my adult life. And then, at long last, it was finally gone. You see, some things—some illnesses, some hurts—take a long time to fully recover from… that's just how it is. You simply can't rush them.

Blessed are the merciful, for they will be shown mercy, Jesus said, as recorded in Matthew 5:7.

So reach out your hand. Have mercy.

Dry the tears that someone's heart may *still* be crying.

Father, let me not judge the length of time it takes for anyone to overcome their hurt. But help me to encourage and believe for the best for them, and not get lost with them in their pain. Let me believe for them that 'this too shall pass' and to not let go of my own faith as I walk with them through a troubled time. Show me how to impart Your hope and love. And help me, too, to always hold onto my faith through any troubled time. In Jesus' name, who suffered but was also filled with joy.

35

A Hero

In Ghana, I went to an International School. It was considered a premier school and was attended by children from around the world. The many flags of the countries we were from hung in large array around our outdoor assembly area. Each day, we stood there at attention in our morning assembly, surrounded by those flags, as the national anthem of Ghana was played. A number of the students were the children of Ambassadors or Embassy-related personnel from around the world. This was true of the only other American in my particular class, an African American young man, who was the child of diplomats associated with our American Embassy.

Though the school was administered by British educators and followed the British system of education, our instructors were from around the globe. Each of my assorted classes was taught by someone from yet another country. My algebra teacher, who we picked up every day on our way to school, was from India—a beautifully dressed woman in her saris of stunning colors and fabrics, and jeweled earrings, necklaces and bracelets. I was intrigued with the various entrancing ways she swept her dark hair up, sometimes with carefully placed strands still brushing her shoulders, and the brilliant red, painted bindi on her forehead.

Our geography class was taught by a Ghanaian man, and we studied the geography of Ghana and surrounding countries. My literature teacher was from England. With her strong accent and exceptionally accurate English, she was intent on making literature interesting but with an emphasis on a much older style of teaching not in vogue in many places even then. But my ability to memorize was honed and stimulated by her teaching style. I still remember standing up and reciting an entire page of small print that I had been instructed to memorize from the little brown book of literature we were using as our text.

I knew little of the British education system. I had never gone to boarding school, only our little mission school for the past years. Here, at our International School, we wore uniforms in an assortment of green colors, ranging from dark to light green. My mother had hurriedly had mine made by a seamstress there in Accra before the first day of school.

On the day I arrived at my new school, I found my way to the only empty desk in the far right corner of the room, which suited me as I was happy to be in a corner, out of the limelight. The open window next to my desk added only heat to the already hot and difficult situation, and the humid air coming through it felt stifling. But, for two days, I sat vaguely contented and hidden in my little corner, trying to get my books organized, get them covered in the requisite brown paper, and learn my classmates' names and the different countries they were from. Next to me was the only other American, the young man from the Embassy. We made a pair: he was taller than I and quite good-looking while I was thin and had glasses and was worried about this new school. Though he did not say much to me, I noticed that he occasionally glanced over at me with what I think he meant as a helpful smile and a bit of a look of sympathy in his eyes.

There was also a growing problem. It became increasingly clear, even in those first few days, that one girl in the class hated me. When we were outside, she would treat me badly, pointing at me, mocking me. I quietly tried to ask around why and always received the same answer: "She hates Americans." She had unfortunately been raised among people who fomented hatred of other countries, especially Americans, and it was spewing out right at me. I had spent the past years of my life in Zimbabwe happily trying to cross many racial and ethnic lines, hour upon hour, day upon day… and now this.

We were into the second week of class when suddenly one day, the teacher loudly called my name from the front of the class, clearly perturbed and quite angry. Her eyes were glaring at me.

"Did you write this?"

The teacher waved a piece of white paper in front of the entire class. I heard very small twittering noises from the direction of my newly self-proclaimed enemy. The class fell silent. Apparently, what was on the paper was revolting. This teacher was strict and known for her punishing ways. Her face was red with fury.

"Your name is on it!" she said angrily. She demanded I come to the front of the class, for disciplinary action, for punishment, which she said would be meted out immediately. I was shaking my head no, I was trembling as I gripped my desk and attempted to rise. Suddenly, with no warning, the young African American boy next to me stood straight up, shoulders squared.

"I wrote it," he announced, back straight, eyes glued ahead. "Don't punish her. Punish me instead."

Our teacher stared at him. The students stared at him. The class was deathly quiet. He had not written it. All the students knew who had written it.

The teacher stood silently for a moment, the paper in her hand.

Was it only a minute that passed? It felt so very long.

"Come with me then," she finally said. And out they went. And yes, he was punished. Instead of me. And instead of the real culprit.

The final part of the punishment she meted out was for him to stand out on the porch outside our classroom in the scorching noonday sun for 30 minutes. It was a dangerous punishment. Many people in Ghana were stricken with sunstroke by that high noon sun, and I doubt the school today would tolerate such behavior from a teacher, and it is my guess that the administration back then may not have known she did it. The students hated that punishment—to stand in shame.

Our class was never quite the same after that. No one ever bothered me. I was not particularly popular; I was mostly scared a great deal of the time. My fellow American and I never became truly close friends, although I think he would have liked to be my friend. But I was far too shy for that. Yet he was always so kind to me and had a friendly smile and nod for me. And always there for me, in the next desk. I could sense that.

In my mind, he has always remained a hero. Someone who saved me. I had done nothing wrong. I was lost. I didn't even understand the parameters of the situation. And there he was. John 15:13 says, *Greater love has no one than this: to lay down one's life for one's friends.* No, he didn't lay down his life for me, but he did stand in the equatorial sun for 30 minutes and spare me public humiliation.

I truly believe that in his heart he felt much more able to bear the punishment than I.

And he may have been right about that.

I know I have never forgotten him.

Father, how do I ever truly thank the people who have been there for me, past and present? What can I possibly say? Like lifeboats in the sea of life they have come through for me, rescued me, listened to me and stood up for me. The apostle Paul says to owe only the debt of love—and I owe that debt to them. Bless them Father. Bless them today.

36

Revolution

Is there a more strangely disquieting and uniquely terrifying sound than that of gunfire in the distance, drawing ever closer?

Soldiers in armed forces live through this repeated exposure for months on end, and there are millions of other individuals— residents of numerous countries—who now live with this terrorizing sound on a daily basis. Every day while some of us just go about our business, they are living in utter terror of explosions and gunfire. They understand on a raw, frightening level those famous words of Psalm 23: *Even though I walk through the valley of the shadow of death* (Psalm 23:4 NASB).

My experience with gunfire in the distance, drawing ever closer, was in Ghana, at the attempted overthrow of the military-run government. My father came downstairs and stood me by the door and said solemnly, his hand on my shoulder, as we heard the gunfire, shouts and clamor in the distance. "You must go upstairs and put all that you can in just one suitcase, he said, "and then come and stay near this door with it, ready to go at a moment's notice when I get back."

With that he left, heading toward the sounds of shouts and yelling.

My mother and I, waiting in the house, got news relayed to us from our Twi-speaking neighbors, who also spoke English, that the airports were shut down, the port closed, and any hope of escape cut off. News flew through our neighborhood that there were possibly even killings going on. Neighbors lined streets and gathered at corners, trying to get updates of what was occurring in the distance.

My mother and I both desperately wanted my father to return, although now our suitcases would be of little use as there were no planes leaving the country. We most certainly would not head north on the roads, given the turmoil, and the ocean stood to the south with no ships available for boarding.

Four hours later, the military forces had regained complete control of the government. But a beloved general had been assassinated.

The general had been instrumental the year before in overthrowing the ruler that some had grown to call a dictator, who had once cared for the people, and had been at the forefront of Ghana's independence from British colonial rule, the first of the African nations to gain independence. But he had, perhaps, too long lived in splendor while many people suffered in abject poverty. At least that is what was told us at the time.

The general and the military had overthrown the dictator the previous year, and now the military itself was the subject of an attempted revolution. We were grateful the coup was squelched and order regained though what life would be like now was yet to be seen.

At that moment, foremost in our minds was that it appeared some sense of safety had returned. The shouting, the gunfire and the terror around us turned to dancing in the streets and bright banners waving from the balconies. Then just as suddenly that, too, turned to anguish and cries as news of the general's death ran like a fire through the country.

Only two months before, at the annual Liberation Day commemoration, people had gathered in happiness and respect. Now, in just days, they would gather again in what has remained the largest funeral gathering I have ever imagined. People flooded the scene of the funeral event, all dressed in brilliant red or carrying something red. Funerals in Ghana tend to be large and sometimes grand affairs, with mourners dressed in red or black, but this was astonishing—a sea of red as far as we could see.

The valley of the shadow of death. The shadow. When that shadow crosses our path everything changes. Sometimes, as in the attempted overthrow of the government of Ghana, the shadow passes, moving away from us as startlingly as it first appeared. Other times, for some of us, that shadow stays, for years, or for months, or for a long night. Still, other times, that shadow turns into a reality. And death is faced.

Today, please say a prayer for those around our planet who are caught in the mind-wrenching terror of gunfire. And for all those caught in the shadow of a child's long illness, the shadow of unexpected bad news or the shadow of financial ruin. Terror is not bound by specifics. It lives in shadow.

Come quickly, God, to help me (Psalm 71:12).

Father, when the shadow of terror crosses my path, give me courage. Courage to stay on the step I am on and not turn to the fear of the future that would encompass me. Give me Your hand to hold. And when I see others caught in the same long shadow of gathering gloom, let me give them my other hand. That way, we are both covered with Your presence. And Lord, we pray for deliverance from all forms of suffering and from evil. We pray that the light and the goodness will return quickly. But whatever the case, keep us with You. In Your Son's name, we do pray.

37

Theft

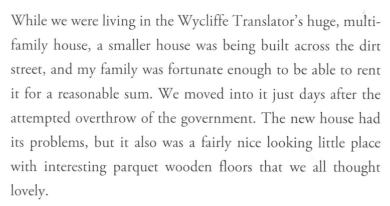

While we were living in the Wycliffe Translator's huge, multi-family house, a smaller house was being built across the dirt street, and my family was fortunate enough to be able to rent it for a reasonable sum. We moved into it just days after the attempted overthrow of the government. The new house had its problems, but it also was a fairly nice looking little place with interesting parquet wooden floors that we all thought lovely.

My mother found some wicker furniture that she used to outfit the living and dining rooms with, and though it was inexpensive, our house really did have the look of an interesting tropical abode. We were a little closer to nature, though, than one might have expected. Beautifully multicolored lizards ran all over the house, both inside and out, as well as a number of spiders. Apparently, it was not exactly what one would term tightly built. We did not know that first night quite how unsecure, but we found out on the second.

As I lay asleep in my new bedroom on that second night, with my belongings scattered here and there, I suddenly awoke. Something had abruptly brought me completely awake, out of a sound sleep. I lay there listening and heard it again—a strange, scratching sound, like something moving.

I swung my legs over the side of the bed and sat, listening. Again, there was a faint scratching sound and more movement. It was coming from the living room. I decided to go across the hall to my parents' bedroom and wake them, then we could walk down that hall to the living room and see what was happening.

I never made it off the bed. I was suddenly immobilized—stopped—in mid-motion. Not in fear. I didn't really know there was anything to particularly be afraid of. And then, the message came.

"You will put your legs back on the bed. You will lie down." I looked around. There was no one standing there, and yet the message was there, in the air. I truly have never known how to describe it. It was not self-generated. It was just in the air, filled with commanding strength.

"You will lie down."

I slowly swung my legs back onto the mattress and lay down, looking around the room, from side to side. I lay there in the darkness, staring at the ceiling. I could still hear movement in the living room but was by now paying no attention. This was far more important, whatever it was.

"You will close your eyes and go to sleep."

I still stared at the ceiling. And again...

"You will close your eyes and go to sleep." It was as though the entire room was saying it.

Slowly I closed my eyes, and, remarkably, went immediately to sleep.

The next morning, I heard my parents talking loudly in the living room. They were clearly agitated. I hurried off my bed and ran down the hallway.

Our new house had been broken in to. The white curtain on the window was blowing in the wind, the window jaggedly broken. Almost all of our mission equipment, which we had just moved over from the Wycliffe Translator's house was gone. So many valuable things—gone. The curtain waved softly over the damage.

That day, my father hired a guard to watch our house during the night. And we began the process of putting huge iron rods over the windows of the house.

Our guard was of the Islamic faith, and I awoke to the sound of his morning prayers coming through the window on many mornings for the rest of my days in Ghana.

The house was never secure from the lizards. We lived with them quite peacefully as they crawled around the inside walls, across tables and floors. But the house was finally secure from thieves. With our huge wrought iron bars over the windows and our wonderful guard, we slept securely at last.

And my lesson was that God can intervene. Like many

others, there have been times in my life when I have felt what I perceived to be God's direction in my life. I have had revelatory thoughts and ideas, and I have felt guidance that seemed to be directly from God. But I had never, and have never since, felt such a thing as happened that night.

Had God granted me the spiritual sight, I do believe I would have seen an angel's outstretched arm in front of me, palm toward me, halting my movement.

And I am grateful. My parents were convinced that I would have been killed had I walked out into that hall with the theft in full progress. There is no way the thieves would have let me live.

In Psalm 91:11, the Bible says that God will give His angels charge of us.

I believe it.

God, I thank You for Your protection. The times I know of it and the times I don't. Have there been a thousand times You have protected me and I didn't know it? Thank You, thank You. Please be with every one of Your people, right now, wherever they are, and particularly be with those in prisons for Your name's sake, or in persecution. Please send an angel to help them.

38

Flood and Danger

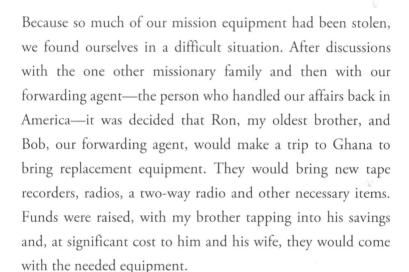

Because so much of our mission equipment had been stolen, we found ourselves in a difficult situation. After discussions with the one other missionary family and then with our forwarding agent—the person who handled our affairs back in America—it was decided that Ron, my oldest brother, and Bob, our forwarding agent, would make a trip to Ghana to bring replacement equipment. They would bring new tape recorders, radios, a two-way radio and other necessary items. Funds were raised, with my brother tapping into his savings and, at significant cost to him and his wife, they would come with the needed equipment.

They had planned on stopping in Israel on their way to see us, as they knew it might be their only chance to see that country, but that part of their flight was abruptly canceled at the very last moment. The Arab-Israeli Six Day War had begun.

The night before they arrived in Accra, it began to rain, and we discovered that not only was the house we had moved to not burglar proof, it was also not waterproof.

I woke to the feeling of water falling on me. Rain was pouring through the ceiling like it was a sieve. The water was inches deep throughout the house. I swung my legs over the side of the bed and heard a splash. In moments, we were up, my mother and father gathering every container to start bailing out our home. We carried the water out as it still rained down upon us from the ceiling. People from the Wycliffe Translator's house arrived from across the street to help. At the end, we were also pushing the water out with large brooms. We did not sleep that night. We only worked, carrying and pushing gallons and gallons of water outside.

Ron and Bob arrived the next day, and we were so excited to see them. They spent time at our little Bible College and met our students there in Accra. They also went to the northern part of Ghana to visit some churches.

My brother contracted an intense tropical illness, possibly a form of malaria, but he fought it valiantly. My father had a policy to eat whatever was put in front of him, no matter how unusual to his own tastes, but on that trip to the north of Ghana he asked the people to please make allowance for my brother as he was still recovering. It turned out the Ghanaian people were very gracious regarding such things, as we would learn they always would be.

It was our intention to show Bob and Ron some of the sights of Accra, even though the attempted coup was still fresh in everyone's mind. On our sightseeing excursion, we walked close to one of the government buildings, housed in one of the old castles near the ocean. Ron was in the middle of taking photos of the old castle by the sea when he found that, as he lowered his camera, he was face to face with a Ghanaian soldier with a loaded gun. The gun was pointed straight at my brother's chest, only inches away.

Tensions were high in Ghana, due to the attempted coup, and the soldier wanted no pictures taken of any government building, as there was great concern about further anti-government plots. The soldier questioned us and then, seemingly reassured, lowered his gun. He confiscated the film as a matter of protocol... but the gun was lowered. He was just doing his duty to protect in a time of high tension, and all was well... in the end.

I've sometimes wondered how my mother survived all these things so well. I know how I survived—I was terrified. But she walked through it all with aplomb and an uncanny assurance. In the course of a few weeks, she had switched countries. She had survived a fire in the Wycliffe Translator's house when a little girl's mosquito netting caught ablaze from the ever-present mosquito coils that burned all night by our beds. She had made it through an attempted government overthrow. Her new home had been burglarized and her daughter's safety threatened. Her home had been completely flooded, with many things ruined, and her oldest son became ill from an intense tropical disease while also having a high-powered rifle pointed directly at his chest. Her other son was far away, and she missed him so.

Yet there she was, putting a nice chicken curry dish and date pudding on the table.

My mother had faith. And what I learned from her is that it's really not quite so much about faith itself, as it is about who your faith is in.

There was danger in the air, those first months after the attempted coup. But that danger passed, unlike the dangers faced by some who have lost everything, some who faced the guns that *were* fired at their chests, not lowered.

On the way back to America, Ron and Bob did stop in Israel—they were on one of the first flights carrying civilians that landed in that country after the war ended.

Tensions were still extremely high there, too, and as they stood at the Wailing Wall they could hear gunfire in the background. They went to Bethlehem, and on the way were stopped because the road had been mined and soldiers were trying to de-mine it. They hired a driver to take them another way, and they were again stopped by soldiers who told the driver to carefully follow his own tire tracks going back as that road also was full of mines.

Guns in Ghana. Guns in Israel and the Middle East. And that was just back then, at one point in time.

There have been so many wars and revolutions, both before and after those days, in so many various places around this world. Many people are caught in them, right this moment.

Perhaps you are caught up in one where you live.

We must press forward together toward peace. And not leave anyone behind. Our planet seems to grow smaller each day, and we are more and more interconnected.

In the Akan language of Ghana, it is called Asmomdwoe. In the Hebrew of Israel, it is Shalom.

And in English… Peace.

And He will be called… Prince of Peace. Of the greatness of his government and peace there will be no end (Isaiah 9:6-7).

Those are the words of the ancient prophet foretelling the time of the Messiah's reign.

That will be a good day.

We continue to pray, Father, for peace. For peace for this earth. For peace in our families. Create in us the hope that we can let go of the walls that divide and reach out our hands in friendship and in Your peace.

39

A Continent, Not a Country

———— ∽ ————

As so many others have said... Africa is not a country, it is a continent. A very large one.

The entirety of the landmass of all of China, all of the United States, all of Europe, and all of Australia combined would easily fit within its borders, with plenty of room for more. It is roughly the same distance to travel from Zimbabwe to Ghana as it is from Anchorage, Alaska, to Berlin, Germany.

Africa has 3,000 distinct ethnic groups and at least 2,000 languages. I have heard it said that some Africans are far more diverse genetically from one another than a Chinese person is from someone of European descent.

It is a continent of diversity. There is snow in Africa, and there is unbelievable heat. What do the Eastern Highlands of Nyanga, in Zimbabwe, a place of woodlands, moors, flowing rivers, and green hills, have to do with the upside down wooden canoes drying out on a sun-drenched beach under swaying palm trees on the Gulf of Guinea, in Ghana?

People around the world, when announcing an upcoming trip, seldom seem to say, "I'm going to North America." They generally say something more specific, as in, "I'm on my way to Canada," or "I'm going to Mexico," or "I'm traveling to the United States." Yet people often just say, "I'm going to Africa," as though it's all one place.

I occasionally find myself speaking that way at times as well, even though I have been in a number of African countries and found that they are different from one another. Thousands of miles apart, nations and cultures developed in unique ways, as is true elsewhere around the globe. Ghana and Zimbabwe, the two African countries that I lived in, are certainly quite different from one another in so many cultural ways.

But there are also some similarities—such as the love of soccer. I watched large groups of boys in Zimbabwe, with only one prized soccer ball between all of them, avidly playing the game, and in Ghana it was also the beloved sport.

Another outstanding thing that Ghana and Zimbabwe shared was the love of movement. Everywhere there is dancing and movement. At our church services in Zimbabwe, people would always dance. They would dance to the front of wherever we were meeting, to put their money in the offering. I loved that.

The same was true in Ghana. The women danced in their beautifully patterned dresses as they brought their offerings forward, their gorgeously colored scarves waving gently from side to side. The men followed next with their offerings, walking together and clapping in rhythm to the music.

The service then came to a stop. The offering money was counted, and if it was not deemed enough to meet the current needs, the entire offering procession started over. It was so straightforward. There was something refreshing about it.

In Ghana, my father and the two other teachers of our little college were graciously invited to travel north to personally meet with the Asantehene, the powerful monarch of the Ashanti (Asante) people, at his Manhyia Palace. They were warmly received. My father spoke well of his conversation with the Asantehene, and they were invited back to visit a few more times. The Asantehene sent gifts with the returning men to be given to their children, and one was to be given to my father's child in Accra, and that was me. It was a pretty, delicate gold necklace in the shape of a flower.

Sometimes the college teachers would go to the north of Ghana to teach classes. Occasionally, they would fly on one of the converted C-47 U.S. Air Force cargo planes that the government had bought and refurbished. More often, though, they would drive up through rainforest areas in the van that belonged to one of the missionaries. It seemed to be our communal car; it was the only vehicle any of us had. Often on those trips through the lush green forest, colorful birds were spotted in the trees and scampering monkeys could be seen swinging from branches.

The missionary teachers were also invited by a prominent

Chief, an Omanhene, to visit him in southeastern Ghana. When they arrived, to their surprise, the meeting room was packed with people, filled with more than one hundred Chiefs from a wide number of places. The Chiefs wore brilliantly colored robes, their linguists by their side, along with their ornately carved linguist staffs. The Omanhene, whose palace they met in, wore a white robe and gold crown. Government officials and news reporters from Accra were also present.

Part way through the meeting, the Omanhene stood up, bringing the meeting to an immediate standstill. To the amazement of everyone, he quoted aloud Proverbs 14:34: *Righteousness exalts a nation, but sin condemns any people.*

I think everyone present was surprised by his words. He said them with such power, such force. As though a wave of truth had gone out. It was a powerful moment in time, carrying almost the weight of a prophetic moment.

He spoke those words, that long ago day, in front of a large group of Chiefs in Ghana.

It is true for Ghana… but it is true for every place. Every country. Every continent.

That Chief's words, quoting the words of a wise king, King Solomon, are for everyone.

Everywhere.

God, give us all the wisdom, whatever nation we are in, to remember the words of wisdom that our nations will only be as strong as they are righteous. And help us know that ongoing sinful activities can only lead to our weakness and downfall. I pray that You will give us the strength to do what we know is right and best, and will make our nations strong in Your sight.

40

The Kingdoms of Africa

The continent of Africa was once a land of great kingdoms. It is only in recent years that the true scope of those long ago empires is finally coming to light. Lost in mystery and time, some lay hidden for thousands of years. Much of the history of pre-colonial Africa, particularly that of sub-Saharan Africa, was concealed and shrouded, some say purposefully, even from many Africans. Most people are only familiar with the pyramids and the history of ancient Egypt.

But there were many other kingdoms.

Kingdoms like the magnificent Gondar, built by the Solomonic Emperors of Ethiopia. With its huge stone castles, its remains are majestic even today. Ethiopia is a land steeped in intriguing history. Documents from the first century rank the old Ethiopian Kingdom of Aksum as one of the four great world powers, along with Rome, Persia, and China. With dynasties starting perhaps as early as 950 B.C., including probable links to the son of Queen Makeda (Queen of Sheba) and King Solomon, many Ethiopians accepted the Torah nearly one thousand years before the advent of Christianity. Thousands of Ethiopians embraced Christianity in the fourth century, and some of the oldest churches in the world are there.

Kingdoms like Wagadou—the Empire of Ghana—with its vast military and legendary wealth. Or the rival Almoravid and Almohad Berber dynasties, competing for their North African Empires.

The Kingdom of Mali was once the second largest in all of Africa and at its height second only to the Mongolian Empire of Asia. Its wealth was exceptional. The Songhai Empire, which emerged from the Kingdom of Mali, was the largest empire Africa has ever seen. In the 16th century, the estimated population of Timbuktu, one of the cities on the Songhai trade routes, was 100,000 people, and was a place where spacious houses abounded, scholarship thrived and weavers of cotton and linen flourished.

The Nubian Kingdoms, the ancient Black Kingdoms of the Nile, have been downplayed for long years. It was the powerful Nubian Pharoah, Taharqa (Tirhakah), King of Kush, who was instrumental in stopping Sennacherib of Assyria from destroying Jerusalem in King Hezekiah's reign (2 Kings 19:9, Isaiah 37:9). Both Greek and Spanish chroniclers maintained that Taharqa advanced into Europe, reaching Spain. Some 3,000 years ago, the poet Homer was purported to have said of Nubians: "They are the most just of men." In the desert of northern Sudan are the Nubian ruins of Meroe, whose wealth came from its robust iron industry—trading with India, China and later Rome. Further north are the ruins of Nubian Kerma, possibly to be numbered among the mightiest cities of antiquity.

The Ashanti Kingdom of West Africa in older days boasted a vast wealth of famous gold, which they traded with many empires. Migrating from the Niger River area, the inhabitants of the Ashanti Kingdom may have descended from the Nubian Empire. They became a powerful and militaristic people with vast plantations and fought wars against colonization. They were weavers of beautiful cloth, builders of interesting towns and cities, and sellers of gold and slaves.

The Swahili, with their picturesque stone cities and glistening shores, were traders from long ago, and the Mesopotamians, the Greeks and the Romans all found their way to the East Coast of Africa for trade. Upon the arrival of Arabs, over 2,000 years ago, the Arab-Swahili people continued to build a powerful trading empire and to be exporters of exotic spices, of gold, and of slaves, brought out to the coast from the interior of Africa. The Portuguese mariner Barbosa, upon landing on the bright shores of East Africa in the 16th century, said, "They dress in very good cloths... with many jewels of gold... and are dressed in silk stuffs."

Old kingdoms, their impact now flowing through the rivers of history.

The Zulu in the south of Africa, believed to have originally migrated from the Congo River Basin, experienced a riveting and sudden rise in military power in the 1800s as a powerful leader transformed the loosely related clans into a single military power. The Zulu Kingdom fought against colonialism and gave the British Empire what is often called the most humiliating defeat in its history before the kingdom ultimately fell to colonial forces.

The Kingdom of Great Zimbabwe, built and inhabited from 1100-1400 A.D., consists of numerous buildings and massive circular walls made of granite stones. The high walls are fitted together with no mortar or mud but have endured for 600 years. It was most probably built by the ancient VaKaranga, ancestors of the Shona people, on lush and fertile land that shows signs of habitation since the first century A.D. The Fortress sits on a hill, far above the tower and enclosure on the plain below. Archaeological findings give evidence that the Kingdom of Great Zimbabwe was rich in gold and was a trading center. Persian glass and Chinese porcelain, as well as Arabian coins from the 13th century, have been excavated on site.

More than once, I have stood in the center of the massive ruins of Great Zimbabwe. All that is left of that distant civilization are the scattered, shattered remains. Everywhere in Africa are the lingering remnants of ancient peoples. Of ancient Kingdoms and dynasties. Ancient civilizations—all gone. But the stories continue, and the ground speaks ...

To walk upon the ground of Africa is to stumble upon land that seems so old, so ancient, that it must have a heartbeat. Like a drumbeat to a very old song.

Wherever we live in this world, we can ask ourselves the same single question: What will history tell of us... of our time? What will it report of our civilization and our particular country?

Will it tell of a warlike people? Or a frivolous people? Perhaps it will tell of a people who frittered away time and resources. A people who were self-centered. Or maybe it will tell of a serving people. A people of esteem and high values who changed the world profoundly for the better and left a legacy, a profound mark upon history for others to follow and be inspired by.

What story will history tell of us? For, eventually, it *will* tell its story. Someday, history will recount the tale of what it sees of us.

When the apostle Paul was in Athens, Greece, he said the following: *From one man He made all the nations, that they should inhabit the whole earth; and He marked out their appointed times in history and the boundaries of their lands. God did this so that they would seek Him and perhaps reach out for Him and find Him, though He is not far from any one of us* (Acts 17:26-27).

The peoples of the past have already had their time, their story. And, civilizations of the future will have their moment of impact, their own place in history. But ours is now. What will it be?

It's an important question. Individuals make up a nation

and a culture. Although at times it seems that those cultures take on lives of their own, it is still groupings of individuals who make up the whole. Our responsibility as individuals is huge—where we choose to speak up and how we choose to live to create the culture around us.

The psalmist David, also an ancient and beloved king, wrote these words: *Therefore, you kings, be wise; be warned, you rulers of the earth* (Psalm 2:10).

We must be warned. We must be wise.

The past kingdoms of this earth, as the dust blows over where they once stood, convict us… we also will pass.

What is our legacy?

Father, there is so much I don't know—about the past, about what ancient peoples thought and what they did. But I do know that our lives, our times, have been handed down from them, handed to us from all who went before us. We have sprung from them. Make us worthy to live up to the best of those who went before us. And let us quickly shed the wrongs of the others who preceded us. Let us find our way, in Your presence, in this time of our lives, to become a beacon for the generations to follow. Help us make them proud to call us their ancestors. Give us the wisdom of old, and the wisdom from above.

41

Slavery

In Ghana, our home was just two or three miles from the beautiful Atlantic coastline. Situated only five degrees off the equator, that coastline is one of swaying palm trees, shallow lagoons, golden sunsets, and blue grey waves crashing on rocks that jut out into the wide sea. Many times I would gingerly climb out onto one of those rocks to find myself surrounded by the beautiful, refreshing ocean spray. Or sit on the coastal sand and watch the fishermen hauling in their wide nets, filled with the day's catch, as generations of fishermen before them had done. Or I would swim far out—too far out—into the churning sea with its strong undertow. That long, long coastline of West Africa is a beautiful sight to see.

It is also the coastline from which wonderful human beings were kidnapped, shackled, raped, tortured and deported by the millions as slaves to Europe, Portugal, Asia, the Caribbean and the Americas. That coastline is one of the most significant and largest stepping off points of the African Diaspora.

The Slave Trade. When Africa was ravaged and used mercilessly. Pillaged. Because, after its resources of diamonds, gold and precious minerals began to not be enough to satisfy, Africa's people were stripped from the land.

One day I sat on the gritty sand, watching the waves, and looked to my left—past the groups of young boys who were supposed to be helping the fishermen but were instead dancing and playing—up to the now whitewashed castle fortress jutting upward on a high cliff, dominating the shoreline. I asked my father, "What is that place?"

He shook his head in sorrow before giving me the answer.

It was one of the European castles that had been erected for the gold trade. Those Europeans had even devised their own name for the area—The Gold Coast. And, then, when adequate gold could not be shipped out, they converted their castles into something that would be used for a different, dastardly purpose—holding grounds for the people they were to sell.

The castles and forts, complete with hideous dungeons, were redesigned to hold humans, who were near starvation but faced the soul-wrenching, shackled walk to the sea to board ships for the Middle Passage. One more horrible, historical embodiment of the Scripture in the book of Revelation regarding those who trade their *cargoes of gold—and articles of every kind made of ivory—and human beings sold as slaves* (Revelation 18:11-13). An unmitigated evil.

It was one of the largest forced migrations in recorded

history.

As I sat on the coast, the blue sea lapping over my feet, and looked up at the old castle fortress through the huddle of laughing boys near the fishing nets, those days seemed, on that lively shore, to be part of an evil, wicked past. One that, in some ways, had receded like an ocean's wave.

Yet, the deep repercussions from those days have never gone away, neither in America nor Africa or elsewhere. We deal with it today as we continue to fight against any institutionalized racism, toward true equality for all peoples, for justice and liberty for everyone. The controversies over how big a part some of the African tribes played in helping the slave traders, by kidnapping and selling nearby tribes, are still being debated, as is how much they actually understood of what terror would befall those tribesmen. There are controversies over how big a part each particular European country played. The castle I was looking at had passed through Danish, Swedish and British hands. The other 30 some forts and castles of Ghana's coast and interior have similar histories, with the first being built by the Portuguese. Then there are the older stories of the Arabian slave traders who over the centuries took even greater numbers of African peoples for the slave trade. Where does it end?

Did it end?

Perhaps that particular portion of the slave trade did end though the consequences linger on with us—many unresolved, and they need to be addressed. But The Slave Trade itself has most certainly not ended.

Twenty-seven million people are currently held in slavery on this planet. And that is the lowest estimate. Millions more, including children, work in sweatshops to produce trinkets or clothing their owners can sell. Thousands upon thousands of girls, women, and boys have been abducted or tricked into slave prostitution. Slave markets exist at this moment, in numerous places, where girls and boys are ruthlessly auctioned and sold into sexual slavery.

How convenient for us if we only pontificate on the despicable wrongs of those past generations without owning the truth of our own times—the place where we actually have a role and a real voice. The one place we can actually make a difference. All written and oral history points to the fact that the people surrounding horrific events did one of three things—they actually bought into and embraced the evil, or valiantly fought against the evil, or they later claimed they just didn't get it, somehow. They just didn't pay attention to what was really happening around them. It sort of crept up on them.

Our moment of power is the present. No one alive today has any decision-making voice at all in what individuals did or didn't do centuries ago. But we do have power—we have a voice—regarding what is going on in our own time.

Where is our voice? How will history judge us? As those who couldn't quite get it? Those who were too busy, perhaps? Or too concerned about our own finances or needs? I wonder what excuse the historians will land on as the central reason so many of us used to justify why we couldn't figure out what to do about the present-day slave trade. Historically, the main reason for slavery is that the goods and services produced from it are so wanted by those using them that they turn a blind eye of convenience on where the goods come from and upon the atrocities perpetrated upon the victims.

There is a castle on the coastline of Africa that stands as a testament to things gone hideously wrong for one people so that another people could have more luxury. Let's not allow history to write the account of our times in the same fashion.

Do to others as you would have them do to you (Luke 6:31). The Scripture is remarkably clear. It needs no explanation whatsoever. So clear that I know I must act, in whatever ways I can figure out. I hope we all do.

Father, help me never to turn the blind eye of convenience on the truth in front of me. Help me never to act as though I just can't quite understand or I don't quite get it, when the true horror of what certain economic systems and greed are imposing on millions of present day slaves is despicable. Help me to find out where the clothes I buy are made. Where the jewelry comes from. What are the practices of the companies making the clothes and the jewelry? How do they manage to sell the goods for just pennies? Help me to have a mind of clarity and sound action and always to be working to be a part of the solution and not a mindless participant in the problem.

42

Where Inaction Ends

Alice Harris changed history.

In 1904, Alice Harris was a missionary in Baringa, in the Congo. British missionaries, she and her husband, John, had been living in that remote area for just a short time when one evening, Alice heard an unexpected knock at the door. With that knock, her world was irrevocably changed.

A Congolese man had made his way in anguish to the missionaries' door to show them what was in the bundle of leaves he clutched with tears to his chest. The severed foot and hand of a small child. The man had failed to meet his weekly rubber quota for the fraudulent and merciless King Leopold II of Belgium, and Leopold's hatchet men had chopped off the hand and foot of his beloved daughter in retribution.

Outraged, heartbroken, and trembling with shock, Alice and John ushered the man inside and heard the unbelievable story. There were no words for the horror. Alice, an amateur photographer, insisted a picture be taken of the atrocity, that the evidence of this hideous action be documented.

John and Alice dropped everything and from that moment, pushed themselves mercilessly, photography equipment in tow, traveling thousands of miles through the Congo River Basin by water and land, over makeshift bridges and through mosquito-infested jungle and grasslands, documenting what they had discovered. Picture after picture captured the images of the brutality, recording in black and white the undeniable truth of King Leopold's Congo.

Leopold had originally presented himself as a philanthropist to the people of the Congo, and disguised his efforts and purposes by saying he would save them from the Arab slave trade. First, he ventured into the sickening ivory business, with its destruction of thousands of elephants, but then something even more lucrative entered his world.

Uses for rubber from the milky sap of the rubber tree had begun to fuel the industrial revolution. Gaskets, valves, seals, and tires were revolutionizing the modern world. Leopold and his emissaries signed hundreds of false treaties with African Chiefs, some of whom rose against him in war when they saw who and what he really was. Meanwhile, his control over vast areas of the Congo was becoming more and more complete as his rubber and ivory empire grew more ruthless.

Alice and John boarded a ship to England and once there showed the pictures of what they had seen. Shockwaves spread across Europe like a wildfire. One of the greatest hidden atrocities of the last century had finally come to irrefutable light, and movement after movement gained traction throughout Europe as people everywhere sought to end the evil. Many scholars maintain that this movement, which grew to international proportions, was the forerunner of all the large human rights movements in the modern era.

Edmund Morel, a shipping clerk working in Antwerp, had also been trying to get the word out. The clerk had uncovered huge shipments of chains and guns going to the Congo and began writing articles in a Belgian journal when he saw only ivory and rubber returning to port. Two missionaries from Virginia, William Morrison and William Sheppard, the first black missionary to the Congo, spoke out loudly and were put on trial inside the Congo itself by Leopold's colonial force. Swedish and Scottish missionaries in the Congo made their way back to Europe at their own risk to offer scathing eyewitness accounts of what they had seen. William Cadbury, the Cadbury chocolate millionaire and Quaker, provided huge financial backing to the movements to end the unspeakable forced labor of the Congo. Booker T. Washington joined the fray. The famous author Mark Twain, already a staunch foe of imperialism, was furious at the news from the Congo and wrote widely read, stinging words about it.

But it was Alice Harris' pictures that traversed Europe and provided the irrefutable evidence. King Leopold II was deposed, losing his throne and all of his holdings in the Belgian Congo, and was seen as a shamed man throughout Europe.

In 1904, one woman living in a remote area of central Africa took one look at something in front of her and knew she must act. Her values were clear. And her immediate action ultimately brought down a king.

What we value matters. There is a right. There is a wrong. And there is a vast difference between the two.

Our world today wants us to think that values are simply shades of gray. But sometimes there is no gray at all. Alice Harris knew this. There was no gray in the severed hand and foot of a small child.

In this world of so-called gray, we risk becoming deceived as to our own power and impact. What can one person do about the modern slave trade? About the suffering children in sweatshops making trinkets? About the other atrocities?

We can do what Alice Harris did. We can do the one single thing, the thing that is right in front of us, whatever that is. Even if it is as simple as writing a letter, or speaking out for the human rights of others, pouring our money into helping those who are in trouble or refusing to buy meat from the place that tortures and abuses animals.

It's easy to dismiss what we could actually do when it's not convenient for us or doesn't seem like enough. But it is only when we do the one thing right in front of us, no matter how small or large, that we carry empowerment. Our action may not end up making the difference we had hoped, but it will certainly make a difference of some sort. And that is what counts.

Alice Harris could not have known whether her pictures would matter. But she valiantly and wholeheartedly traversed the Congo River Basin and took the action in front of her, because it mattered to her.

What we value matters.

Many years ago, my sister-in-law shared with me a Scripture that had been meaningful to her and to my brother Jim. *If anyone, then, knows the good they ought to do and doesn't do it, it is sin for them* (James 4:17).

That Scripture has stuck with me over the years. I think of it quite often. It's a very personal Scripture. It says that when a person is aware of what matters—what is right—and doesn't take action, for *that person* it is sin.

It always makes me ask the same question: What thing in front of me do I know is right to do, the right action for me to take? What matters to me?

And so I will ask you this same question. What matters to you?

Father, forgive me for the numerous times I have taken no action. When I have used not knowing what to do as an excuse to do nothing. When I have thought my actions too insignificant to matter and chose inaction instead. Forgive me for not fully reckoning that my actions, whether known or unknown, do matter, that my action may be the one that opens the eyes of countless people. Or of a few people. Or of no one at all, but only seen by You. Forgive me for inaction. Forgive me for selfishness. In Jesus' name, the one who bought that forgiveness for me.

43

Chess

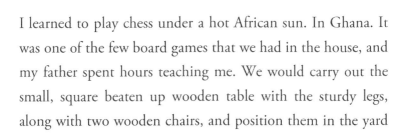

I learned to play chess under a hot African sun. In Ghana. It was one of the few board games that we had in the house, and my father spent hours teaching me. We would carry out the small, square beaten up wooden table with the sturdy legs, along with two wooden chairs, and position them in the yard as near the tree as possible so we at least had some shade from the glaring sun. And we would play our game of chess.

My father, who had meticulously taught me the names of the southern sky constellations on dark, starry nights in Zimbabwe, and who thought that the Koine Greek language was a useful thing to teach a ten-year-old, now set about teaching me, by the hour, how to play chess. A highly busy man, gone for hours to do mission work, he made sure to take some time out in the late afternoon to teach me something. For many months, that something was chess.

My father, who had grown up in unusual and hard

circumstances, seemed to pay scant attention to the theory that one is only capable of learning certain things at certain ages. He could somehow teach anything in an age-appropriate way—it was a gift that he had. He simply taught whatever was in front of him to teach, at whatever age I happened to be at the moment. We often read large chunks of the encyclopedia together, and he made it seem enthralling. We had an old phonograph, and he had some records of various operas, so we enjoyed those too. Today's views that kindergarten children can learn three languages at once would have made perfect sense to him.

For weeks, my father sort of played both sides of our chess board, playing his own while giving me his best suggestions and thoughts on how to play my side. Sometimes he let me make the move without any aid; at other times, we plotted together what my best moves would be. He was as delighted when my side won as he was his own, and I can still hear that characteristic laugh and joy at my win.

But then the day came, one hot afternoon under the tree, when he looked across the little wooden table with a glint in his eye and said, "I'm not going to just let you win anymore." The initial training was over. We would now play for real.

I always felt like I somehow grew up that afternoon. Not that there wasn't a lot of growing up left to do, but I cannot forget the strange feeling that overcame me. I had to fight for my side of the board now. It was mine to win or lose.

What happened next was that I lost countless games in a

row. All the games, in fact, for the next months. But my spirit wasn't broken. The teaching now came after the game, going back over what I could have done, finding better-thought-out strategies.

But then the day came when I won my first game of chess. Even now, I wonder if my father was not distracted with work that day, but whether he was or not, I won, fair and square. And he hadn't let me. His excitement at my win was as great as my own.

I wonder if sometimes God doesn't teach us the way my father taught me. Intense one-on-one at the beginning. And then having us stand on our own a bit. At least not rehashing over and over only what we have already learned.

Maybe we are expected to kind of hold onto those initial steps ourselves. We're never on our own with God—we can't do any of His work or follow His will without His power running through us, without the Holy Spirit's power charging our efforts. He made the air we are breathing.

But perhaps, sometimes, we don't acknowledge the fact that we are expected to hold firm on the things we've already learned, to sort of stand on them with some of our own strength, while He pushes us on to learn other, different things.

I went on to win a few more chess games with my father, though not many. My father was a very good chess player.

I was never one of the best; I've been beaten at chess many times. But what mattered is that I had learned, and I could play remarkably well for my age.

The one thing I have not forgotten about chess is that it's necessary to think ahead, to plan and consider options. It was ingrained in me all those afternoons in the sun as we played, brushing sweat from our foreheads and drinking our glasses of water. And while I may still need to learn a lot more about the importance of forethought—in fact, I know that I do—I have not lost the basic principle.

And maybe that, too, is what God does when He teaches us. He wants it ingrained. Not so much the details of every situation we go through, but the principles, the concepts, what we learned and what we can take from those situations.

Perhaps something along these lines is what the writer of Hebrews was thinking when he wrote with some frustration to his readers: *In fact, though by this time you ought to be teachers, you need someone to teach you the elementary truths of God's word all over again. You need milk, not solid food!... But solid food is for the mature, who by constant use have trained themselves to distinguish good from evil* (Hebrews 5:12-14).

I know I need to keep holding on to what I've learned and also keep growing.

May God help us all... to grow up a little more each day.

Father, help me to stand firm on what I have already learned about Your word, about Your ways and about You. I don't want all You have taught me in my life to be in vain. I don't want You to have to keep re-teaching me what You and I have already gone through. I want to hold on to it. I want to build from that base. I want to go forward. I want to incorporate Your teachings and move ahead to more understanding. Let me not be as one who looks in the mirror and goes away, forgetting what he saw, but as one who is a doer, not just a hearer.

44

What I Learned from the Traders

The road in front of our house in Ghana was a dirt road, and many a day I would look up and see a tall figure, with a flowing white robe and turban, walking down the dusty road, stopping here and there to talk to people. One of the Traders.

Many of the Traders appeared to be from Nigeria, but some were from Ghana itself. They carried their wares in a large fabric sack slung over their shoulders, and they stopped and dealt with anyone who had the slightest interest. Many people waved them on. No time to trade with the men walking the town with their goods for sale.

But, I would deal as they called it. They seemed to find the singular focus of a young girl, now with coffee-bean skin and highly sun-bleached hair, intriguing. And I also had a bit of money.

My accent by that time sounded as though I originated from England, so that seemed confusing to them, as I staunchly maintained that I was an American. Cross-legged or on a little wooden stool, I sat at the edge of the blanket they had spread on the ground, the Trader on the other side of the blanket and all of his wares spread out between us, ready to stay for thirty minutes or so. They would not give up on me—probably because they knew, in the end, I would buy something, even if it were small. And I, too, didn't give up on getting something at a price I could afford, which indeed was quite small. I still have part of my collection of small mahogany carvings and pretty beaded bracelets and rings.

My mother used to ask me how I could stand the back and forth haggling over the price. I did it because I enjoyed their company and the laughter.

Also, because it was my one chance to buy something at a price I could pay. We were often down on the streets of the merchants in Accra, especially the lines of shops where our Indian friends and numerous others had stores. These were all stores that opened onto the street, with strong, heavy iron gates that were pulled across the front at night. The stores themselves went far back from the opening, large rectangular rooms, some almost dark at the back or lit by lamps. Accra was a port city, and these were import shops.

But I couldn't afford anything there, even though I loved drinking mineral water or sipping the beautifully spiced tea as I sat on the rug on the floor while my parents visited. In one store, I was surrounded by gorgeous handwoven rugs, and other beautiful items from India, carved from teak, and beautiful vases, plates, jewelry and copper items. In the store we went to most often, there were numerous items of clothing, luggage and shoes for sale in every corner of the store. Our friends from India, who owned the luggage and clothing store, made us feel almost like their family. They really liked my parents, and their shop was a pleasant place for us to visit.

It was also one street over from the long rows of red mailboxes, hundreds of them, that went on for blocks and served as the way to get mail in Accra. Across from the mailboxes, people sat at tables with typewriters in front of them and umbrellas over their heads to protect them from the boiling sun. They were clerks, and they would type things for a fee. Going to downtown Accra to get our mail was an important task we did at least twice a week.

Though I could not afford anything at the Indian import shops, with the Traders, I had a business. It was clear that they would never go below their lowest price. But it was also clear that I had to get them to a price I could afford. So we would haggle, back and forth, raising our arms in disbelief at the newest price, laughing when we finally came to agreement— "You got the better deal." "No, no you did! You have bested me this time around!"

As it says in Proverbs, *"It's no good, it's no good!" says the buyer—then goes off and boasts about the purchase* (Proverbs 20:14).

The Traders could often see the change in my hand so they generally knew how much I had. And I seldom had more; I simply didn't. It was a game—it was a shrewd business. It was important to them to sell their wares, and it was important to me to feel like I had a place I could actually buy something.

But then a rather eye-opening thing happened. I realized that we didn't need to just use money. I could trade a bracelet I no longer wanted or liked for a bracelet a Trader was selling. Suddenly, the world opened, for we were no longer bound by the monetary system.

Many of the Traders who came down our road were regulars. I grew to recognize them, and I knew their names.

The selling and buying of things was a big business in Accra. The huge markets, with vendors set up under umbrellas, in stalls or in the open air were a sight to see. I don't know how long it would have taken to walk entirely through all of the market in downtown Accra, but if you did it seems you could find almost anything: women grinding peppers, stacks of smoked fish, stews, rows of spices, stacks of bread loaves, vegetables and fruits of many kinds—unbelievably fresh pineapple, and the alasa fruit that I have never seen anywhere else. There were meats, household items by the thousands, garments, colorful fabrics, scarves, headdresses—the list felt endless. And, of course, the country is the second largest cocoa bean producer in the world. Accra—and Ghana as a whole—had a lively feeling to it. Commerce, it seemed, was in the air.

Women in Ghana were attuned to business. Our original little college building was rented from a Ghanaian business-woman. A number of the tribes of Ghana were matriarchal, meaning that the lineage was passed down through women.

There were also people who just came walking down streets, generally also women, with huge baskets balanced on their heads, selling their goods—piles of peanuts in the baskets or high piles of fresh bread or fruits.

Street food in Ghana is an interesting assortment of countless items, whether yam chips, fresh pineapple (often picked that day) or amazing fresh seafood sold at stands on the beach. I like the idea of walking out the door and stopping the girl going by, giving her some change, and walking away with a handful of peanuts or some other commodity.

I have never been able to learn the exact history behind the white-robed Traders of Ghana and Nigeria: how the whole concept of walking down roads with one's wares to sell ever started. I have heard different theories about it. And that makes sense, I guess, because as is true with most vocations, people are doing them for different reasons. Some are honest; some are not. Some didn't come by their goods rightly; some did. True of Wall Street, true of the local car dealers... true of the Traders, I would imagine.

What I learned from the Traders is that there is more than one way to earn a living. More than one way to do something. That piece of information has come in very handy for me through the years.

I find that I like to support people who have little businesses they have started: entrepreneurs who try to drum up income to support themselves. Homemade jewelry businesses; fish sandwich shops started out of a kitchen; food stands on the college campus run by college kids, or even people selling homemade cakes and cookies to friends out of their home. Sometimes it's a homespun business hurriedly put together in desperation due to lost jobs or the need to help a child through college or sometimes just to simply earn extra money.

Some say these little businesses are irrelevant, that they won't support someone through the long-term, that they lack a long-term strategy.

But they matter, and I like to support them because I know it might help somebody get through this week.

And there are parts of this world where that's a very big deal.

Father, I ask that You will always provide livelihood for those I love and for all of Your people. Help all of us to be willing to do whatever is before us, without worry as to the status or value attributed to it. Help us to value the real meaning of productive work. And be glad when we have it. And be glad for food on our table for one more week. And for this day.

45

Stories and Proverbs

Like so many places, Africa abounds in stories and proverbs, passed down from the distant generations. And, like the stories from other places, many of Africa's stories carry the universal messages that teach us how to live or show us anew a realization about our world. Stories of people, or animals, who get what they deserve. Warnings to beware of tricksters. Stories that emphasize the importance of learning from past mistakes. Stories with an unexpected twist at the end that sharply remind us to be careful in our judgments because everything may not be as it first appears. Stories of the sorry price to pay for greed or envy. And hundreds upon hundreds of proverbs, or short sayings, that imbed in the mind a particular truth, warning or realization.

Jesus used parables and stories to drive home his points for a reason—because we remember them.

I have known individuals who say they haven't opened a

Bible in years—or ever. Yet upon hearing the words, "the Story of the Good Samaritan," they immediately reply, "Oh, I remember that one!"

Interesting.

Stories transport us as the images evoked rise up in our minds, yet we remain grounded in our seats. We grow entranced with the plot, no matter how small or simple, as the message of the story seeps into our awareness. We want to know what happens next. A group of children sitting cross-legged in a small circle, intently listening to a story being told, seem identical in their demeanor and interest across the globe. Whether they are at a scouting campfire in Colorado, a village fire in Zimbabwe or an igloo in Alaska, their eager eyes glow in anticipation as the story unfolds.

Africa's stories and proverbs carry a distinctive African flavor, just as those from China carry a particular feel or those from Russia really do seem Russian. But, given that Africa is such a huge continent, there are wide diversities as well. Some, like the Anansi spider stories, seem to be told in some form in many countries across the continent.

One of my favorite proverbs is an old Shona proverb that states: "He who warns you is your friend."

One of my favorite stories is from the Zulu people, a story about a time after the days when The Greatest One—the Creator—had made humanity, but not too long after First Man and First Woman had walked on the earth together. It is the story of their descendants. It tells how these descendants were sad because they did not know the ancient stories to tell their children. Finally, after a series of adventures, the inhabitants of the underwater Sea Kingdom gave one of them an exquisite and beautiful sea shell that, when held to the ear, softly whispered the tales of long ago.

We spend our years as a tale that is told, is how the King James translation renders Psalm 90:9. I wonder, sometimes, what my story will be.

I listened to a speaker tell a story the other day, and it was flawless. Afterward, I wondered how many times he must have practiced it, how many times he must have honed his speaking skill, to make it seem so succinct and fluid. Not a single misstep. And it reminded me of the older people groups who placed such a value on the oral tradition of passing on stories. We have lost most of that; we have little understanding of memorizing each and every word and making sure it gets transmitted to the next generation perfectly. Some Middle Eastern and African cultures have handed down stories utterly intact, by memory, for hundreds upon hundreds of years.

There is an old African proverb that says: "When an old man dies, a library burns to the ground." I think it is especially appropriate that it is an African proverb, for the African people traditionally respect their elders.

Jesus used so many different teaching styles. His most important may have been the straightforward way he simply relayed truth and spoke of the reality of who he is. Those statements are clear-cut and to the point. The miracles themselves were profound statements that showed and undergirded this truth, showing us that he could back up what he said.

In addition, he taught us by his actions. He did not shun the woman at the well with five husbands. He did not hesitate to stand up to the false teaching of the Pharisees. And then, as if all of that straightforward speech and truth were not enough, he taught us with the parables and the stories.

Jesus told this parable: *A farmer went out to sow his seed. As he was scattering the seed some fell along the path... Some fell on rocky ground... Other seed fell among thorns... Still other seed fell on good soil...* (Luke 8:5). Nearly every culture on earth can follow the gist of this story and how the state of the soil mattered. An African farmer, an American farmer or a farmer in Finland all grasp it immediately.

Jesus also told this small story: *The kingdom of heaven is like treasure hidden in a field. When a man found it, he hid it again, and then in his joy went and sold all he had and bought that field* (Matthew 13:44). Around the planet, people quickly understand the meaning of finding something of such extraordinary value.

He taught them many things by parables... (Mark 4:2).

I think we are fortunate that he did. Around this globe, from Africa to Australia, we can all latch onto the story.

We listen to stories. We instinctively try to figure out what they mean.

But then Jesus understood that. He understands us.

Jesus, what will the story of my life be? How will it go? Give me the wisdom to want it to be a story of meaning, a story that helps others and that honors You. I know that sometimes stories have difficult moments, happy moments, troubled moments, suspenseful moments, bittersweet moments. Some end early and some last long. But in the end, just make mine count. Make it count somehow. For You.

46

Harmattan

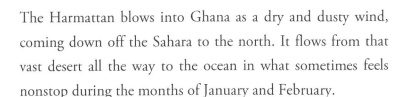

The Harmattan blows into Ghana as a dry and dusty wind, coming down off the Sahara to the north. It flows from that vast desert all the way to the ocean in what sometimes feels nonstop during the months of January and February.

For me, a dusty dryness did not feel like a particularly new thing after the dry season of Zimbabwe; however, there is something quite different about the Harmattan. People have asked me if I have been to the Sahara Desert, and I always reply that although my father traveled through parts of it, I did not. I did, however, taste it, feel it, and brush it off my skin. For the Harmattan carries the dust of the Sahara.

There are times when the storms of life come as a dry and dusty time. A dryness that just goes on, seemingly endless. A time when the songs don't sound the same. When the music has long disappeared.

A time when dreams are shattered, lives changed, and roads

redirected.

These are the wrenching times, the times we come close to losing our lives, or even do. The times of agony. The times of wailing.

The hardest thing to believe, at those times, is that God is with us. That there is something larger than our present.

I see Hagar, the Egyptian, in the desert, desolate, thirsty, crying out to God for her son, Ishmael. For his thirst, for his life. The country she was traveling through, as she tried to go home, was brutal; a tormenting, arid landscape. It's startling she survived. I see Joseph, thirteen long years in an Egyptian dungeon prison, waiting for hope. Sold by his own brothers and forgotten, even, by the fellow prisoner he helped. We are told God was with them both.

Hagar's son's name meant "God has hearkened." I think that is the hardest thing to believe in the desert, in the dry, dusty land as one cries for help. That God has hearkened.

What God provided Hagar was a spring of water.

And that is what we all need in those debilitating times. A spring of hope, of water, of life, of a future.

Sometimes we can barely survive the storms. Other times we are surprised at our own resilience and by the extraordinary mercies of both God and our fellow humans.

The Bible says, of Hagar, that an angel came to her, and, *God opened her eyes and she saw a well of water. So she went and filled the skin with water, and gave the boy a drink* (Genesis 21:17-20).

And with that action, life went on.

There are those who live their lives in the desert, entire peoples who have learned to live in the desert, for thousands of years. They have made a life for themselves in some of the most difficult places on earth. And there are people around me now who have learned to survive even though things continue being very hard for them.

The Harmattan did carry one nice thing with it, the temperatures in Accra fell at night. Still, I personally didn't like the taste of desert in my mouth. Or that gritty feeling of sand in my eyes.

I don't think most people do. It might serve us all well, then, to not judge anyone going through desert days, through their journey of hardship. Perhaps instead, we could try to be an oasis for them. An oasis in their desert.

Perhaps we should have a hands-off policy in terms of judgment. It is the worst of all times to judge them. It is, instead, a time to remember Jesus' statement: *Do not judge, or you too will be judged* (Matthew 7:1).

And a hands-on policy to do all we can to help. To pray that God will hearken. To provide the spring of hope if we can. And if we can't, again, to cry out for them as Hagar, the Egyptian, cried to God. That He will hearken.

———✍———

God, I pray that You will bless and help the people on this earth who are walking in a desert place, whether a physical desert or a spiritual one. I pray that You will hearken to their cry. You will provide the living water for them. And You will show us all how to be an oasis in the desert for each other, a place to weather the hard times of life.

47

My Father

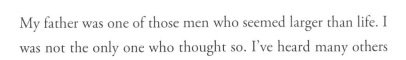

My father was one of those men who seemed larger than life. I was not the only one who thought so. I've heard many others make that statement about him over the years.

It would take volumes to recount all he ventured out to do.

He floated down the Nile River, with hippos swimming by the small boat. He walked on little-known roads in India. He loved preaching in the Appalachian hills. He went into dangerous countries, to people meeting in fear from their governments to spread the gospel he so loved. He had seven college degrees. He was brilliant, in a way few people seem to be. He seemed to know history by heart. Just name a country, name an era. He used to sit and work out math problems just for fun in the evening, to pass a leisurely moment. His enjoyment of life was contagious. He loved to watch cartoons and read Disney books with his grandkids, whom he adored, every single one of them. He had a great laugh and gave the best hugs.

My father had deep experience with pain and poverty. He was a first-generation converted Christian, not born into a Christian family. Abandoned by his own father, he went hungry and barefoot and began work in the steel mills at the age of ten to help support his mother and younger brothers and sisters. He personally experienced the impact of horrifying crime and abuse around him, and it is the grace of God that his life turned out as it did. He always said that with great certainty.

At the age of twelve, he wandered into a church he saw while walking alone down a Chicago street. He had felt inwardly compelled to enter. He sat at the back, looking around, and it was at that moment that an elder at the front of the church saw him and came to that back row and sat down next to him, to inquire and talk with him. The deacons and elders of that church took one young boy under their wing and began to help him in his miserable circumstances, to encourage him, and history changed.

Later they wanted to enroll him in a mechanics school, as he had shown an aptitude and love for both carpentry and mechanics. They hoped for at least some education for him. But they were unaware even then of what he was capable. He, instead, was determined to go to a four-year college, no matter what it took or how hard he had to work, so he set off with one suit and pair of shoes in an old suitcase. My father ended up teaching Latin and Philosophy, along with numerous other subjects. He spoke five languages and was capable of getting around in two others. People flocked to him just to talk with him because he had a startlingly clear discernment. He had a kind heart. My mother said she had watched him give away his last ten dollars in order to help someone.

He was that unique person who is quite at home in a castle or at a pauper's table. I don't know why, exactly. He just saw the people and not the surroundings. He believed in people, their capabilities and their uniqueness.

My father felt strongly about treating people well and with equality. Years before we ever left our Tennessee home, he had already gotten himself into tremendous hot water on that subject. As a pastor, he had invited all the members, leaders, the pastor, elders and deacons, along with the choir of the local black church to come and worship with us in our all-white congregation, well before the days of desegregation in the South. He did it because he believed it was right. And that's how he was. My parents and I were far away in Africa during the height of the American Civil Rights Movement, but I knew well where my father stood on those things because he had already taken his stand.

Probably the one thing I would hope to ever pass on from my father, if I could, was the way he made people think. Over and over, he pushed me to think. "Never assume, and never presume. Always, always think." It's what he taught us all, I guess. To always think.

I often hear people despair of only impacting one life. They bemoan their small circle, their short reach. They feel small or lacking because they have lived in one place all their life, that they have only a few friends. They lament that they have never done "great" things. I could not disagree with them more. I think of that elder who had the wherewithal to walk to the back of a church that snowy Chicago morning and help a young barefoot, ragged, sad boy, utterly abandoned by his father. That man changed history. I will never know him unless by a miracle. I don't know his name. But I will tell you this. There is no way to put any price on how that elder and those deacons changed history. They changed my history and that of my family.

My father's gift was that of a teacher. He taught me the names of the stars at night, meticulously finding them on the star map and having me memorize them in the sky. He taught me the dynamics of how airplanes fly for the simple reason that we happened to be flying on one. He taught me to think. On and on, every day. He taught constantly, everywhere we went. At heart, he was a teacher.

My father's greatest message in life was that God is real. The saving gospel of Jesus and the truth that there is a God was his heart blood. That message still echoes down the lives of all who knew him. My father preached that gospel, the good news, of the Messiah Jesus around the world. He went to so many places after the Africa days, to relieve missionaries in various locales by taking over their work for them when they needed a break. He went into dangerous places, behind the Iron Curtain. He went to plant churches in remote places where there had been none, and in places where the church had existed for centuries and was in trouble. He was instrumental in starting many mission works in entire regions where people had never heard the gospel.

It is a long list—the places he went and the work that he did, while also continuing on as a university professor teaching World Religions and also Missions and Bible subjects. Much of the rest of his life was spent traveling the world preaching the good news of Jesus.

His favorite song was "Amazing Grace."

When he became sick, calls poured in from around the world, people we did not even know from nations most of the family had never been to. So many, in tears, telling us how he had changed their lives. He was buried with a handmade blanket from a tribe in northern India. They had called in tears and asked that it be put in the casket as a special thank you from them. A family from China made a journey to his grave to show their gratitude and to play their violins in his honor on the windy hillside over his tombstone.

If you ever happen to see any lost and barefoot, hungry children wandering around, in any part of the world, don't overlook them. Please. Believe me, they matter. Take it from me… they may matter to many people in the very long run. And I assure you with tears, they matter to God. This is one thing I know in life and am sure of. Because once my father was one of those lost boys, and he mattered. He mattered to me.

Jesus said: *I was hungry, and you gave me something to eat, I was thirsty and you gave me something to drink, I was a stranger and you invited me in, I needed clothes and you clothed me… Truly I tell you, whatever you did for one of the least of these brothers and sisters of mine, you did for me* (Matthew 25:35-40).

My father mattered to me.

———————

Father, You see the person. You don't judge our value by poverty or wealth. You don't put us in a category by our nationality or our race. You don't judge us by our social or education level. You always see the person. Help me to see people that way too. Help me to know in the depths of my understanding that every human being, and all of life, has extreme value. Don't let me overlook anyone. And thank You for not overlooking me. We pray in Jesus' name, who gave his life for us all.

48

My Mother

My mother was one of those women who other women really liked. But both women and men and young people, sort of gathered round her wherever we went. Though I could name a hundred reasons why that might have happened, in the final analysis, I think it was because she radiated an interest in people that was quite uncontrived. She had an acceptance of them and a somewhat unexpected sense of humor.

Even when she was ninety, she would still reach out from her wheelchair and sort of pat people's hands, holding them for a minute, looking into their eyes with such a sweet expression and smile of concern for them. She also had a straightforward way of talking, yet always laced with a southern kindness that was remarkably endearing. I have known no one else who could tell you to your face you were doing something wrong and somewhere inside yourself you knew you had also heard "I love you."

We went through a lot together, my mother and I.

I don't think my mother would ever have thought of going to Africa. In fact, I'm sure of it. I don't believe she had ever intended to go anywhere too far outside the foothills of the Appalachians. She was born on Cherokee land, less than an hour's drive from what would, some twenty years after her birth, be formally christened the Great Smoky Mountains. She was from people well-known in the area, a large and caring family, and they had deep and grounded roots there. They were beacons of light for many people, including us. They had taken in orphans; they had clothed and fed the poor. Before I was born they had, in great faith, sold off their crops to pay the first preacher of the church in their area so he could have a salary.

My parents were as different as day and night in so many ways and were from profoundly different backgrounds: he from a severely broken family and she from a deeply stable one. But in ways that counted, they were remarkably the same. They both loved God with all of their heart, and that single fact defined their lives. They both connected well with people, and people were drawn to them. They greatly loved each other. It has made me ponder, from time to time, if it is the similarity in the truly important things that makes a marriage work and not the superficial qualities of income or backgrounds.

My father often said, in very certain terms, that after the foremost saving grace of God in his life, this woman's love and prayers also saved him.

I can still hear her voice teaching African women on my

veranda, the porch that was attached to my bedroom. Why my veranda was chosen for that, I don't know, but that eventually became its designated purpose during the day.

At the end of her life, in addition to her years in Africa, my mother had been in forty-two countries. She had met with and encouraged countless missionaries in various countries and had many international students in her home, both to live and as friends. She had personally taught the English language to students from China and India in her home, and had been part of a groundbreaking ministry team for emerging pastors from Romania when it was still under communist control.

When I go to bookstores these days, and see all the sections of self-help books, I sometimes just shake my head… I wish they could have just gone and talked to my mother. She seemed to know those theories without studying them—theories about the importance of community and engaging life in the present. She understood the value of community, and one formed around her wherever she was, somehow without her ever leaving behind the ones she already had. And she understood about living in the present. No matter what happened, she stuck with the fact that we are where we are, and she tackled that with gusto.

She had a smile that lit up the room.

Right after she passed on, she got a call that came to my phone instead, from an African lady who had lived on our mission station in Zimbabwe, a person whom my mother dearly loved. The woman was in America visiting one of her sons who was studying to be a doctor. Every time she came to America to see him, she had made a long-distance bus trip just to sit and visit with my mother in her retirement home, and she was hoping to come and see her again.

My mother would have been so sorry to miss that call.

My mom was always intrigued that I tended to remember details, of events and locations, from our many experiences both in Africa and other places while she remembered the people.

With her, it was always the people.

No matter how far she went and how many wondrous and interesting things she saw or experienced, she remained, at heart, a warm-hearted Southern girl with faith, who truly loved others. She could remember individuals I had long forgotten. By her bed, still hanging there on the bedpost after she passed away, was a little plaque that said, "Love Spoken Here." Of all the sayings floating around, that's the one she chose to have near.

Wherever we were in the world, for those many years, when she spoke of "home" it always meant East Tennessee.

I have always hoped for her sake that some small corner of heaven looks like her beloved East Tennessee.

She would simply love that.

———✧———

God, I thank You for my mother.

49

Mistakes Were Made

I don't understand people who say they have no regrets. I have many... Things I wish I had said or done... Actions I wish I had taken. From our time in Africa, through the rest of my life, up to this present moment. But, I don't live in regret because that would seem stagnating. We must forgive ourselves and others. We simply must go forward.

But to have no regrets? I can't imagine.

I'm sure that we made mistakes when we were missionaries. The reason I am so certain of it is that all human beings make mistakes, except our Lord Himself. But tremendous good occurred as well. I know that because of the numbers of African people who have said so. My parents, along with many of the other missionaries, were loved and respected there, and I think it's because their hearts were right, and the people around us picked up on that. People in general across this planet have the interesting ability to intuitively understand when someone is trying to do things well and with integrity, whether they make mistakes or not. And, also, to intuitively know when that is not the case.

It meant so much when a high-ranking member of the Ghanaian government at the time told one of our fellow missionaries that the reason he and other government colleagues enjoyed spending time with us and helping us succeed was that we were unlike some other missionaries of the time. He said many Ghanaians could sense that they were merely being tolerated by some missionaries, but that they did not feel that from our little group. From us, he felt a genuine respect and love.

By far, the missionaries we lived among were exemplary people. Some had given up lucrative careers, they had spent their savings, they were apart from loved ones. Some gave almost their entire adult lives to this purpose, and they did it with grace and cheer. To this day, I feel like standing when they enter a room. My respect for them and what they accomplished is strong and high. A number of the adult children and even the grandchildren of those missionaries continue to serve the people of Africa today, founding orphanages and schools.

But, as with all groups of people, missionaries are not a homogenous lot. All people do whatever they are doing and go wherever they are going for widely diverse reasons. The same was, and is, true of missionaries. Some of the earliest missionaries had gone to Africa as part of a growing colonialism;

others, from the very same time period, were distinctly separate from it. Some lost their lives opposing that colonialism, killed by their own countrymen far from home. They had come with a far higher purpose, a far nobler mission.

But, it is so sad to say, there were some for whom this was not the case. And looking back at their presence has made me understand the stories I've heard about the great damage done by such types of people.

I've never figured out why they came, quite honestly; it must have been for some strange reason of their own. We had a few run-ins with them, and both of my parents were distressed at their lack of honoring the people around us, their lack of honoring the people's way of life and the dignity of their personhood. I am happy to report they were not the majority.

It came to mind one day to wonder if this anomaly is still going on around me, where I live now. Instead of looking back, I decided to look around. And yes, I found it. Individuals, from all walks of life and every political corner, who are helping the hungry or working on some other worthy endeavor. Yet even while engaging in such worthy tasks, they seem filled with resentment and anger at their fellow human beings who are also helping others in the exact same way. Even hateful most of the time, these 'aid-givers' mock and demean those whom they deem to not be right—in other words, those who do not agree with the mocker's personal political stance or beliefs. Worse, sometimes the disgruntled helpers even put down those they are supposed to be aiding.

Then there are also those individuals who choose to only pontificate about social issues, at great length, instead of actually doing something. Whatever that seed of resentment and discontent is, it carries a negative life force that gnaws at the individual and threatens to poison those around them.

One thing that I had to learn early on in life is that very often people who are not doing much of anything will relentlessly criticize those who at least had the guts to get out there and try. It was a hard lesson, then and now. It is just a price that the risk takers pay.

The Bible states in the book of James, *For we all stumble in many ways…* (James 3:2). And that is simply the case, no way around it. Yet that same book also says, *If any of you lacks wisdom, you should ask God, who gives generously to all without finding fault, and it will be given to you* (James 1:5).

So I guess that is the key. Since we're all apparently going to be making mistakes, and there seems to be no way around that fact, then the way through it is to, many times a day, ask God for wisdom. Wisdom to avoid the mistakes altogether, to mend the mistakes we have already made and to quickly own up to the ones we may make this very day.

In the end, it seems that all we can do is lay everything at the feet of Jesus and ask him to bless it. To fix our errors and to amplify the good that was done. Then, to let go and let it all flow into the great river of life. And pray that the good survives.

My dad used to say, "We need wisdom to get through this day."

No particular explanation. Just the statement, and on he would go.

The older I get, the more I find myself saying that, too.

<hr/>

Father, forgive me for my mistakes. But mostly, forgive me for the times I willfully did wrong. The mistakes? Well, You and I both know, they were just mistakes. More serious are the times I knew better. But nevertheless, please don't let even my mistakes hurt others. That is the worst thing of all—when I have hurt others and didn't mean to. Please intervene. Please solve the outcomes of my mistakes. You will have my eternal gratitude.

50

Values

For centuries, throughout much of Africa, cattle were considered extremely important. Though teeming with diverse wildlife, the continent's old caves and stones bear the images of cattle more than any other animal. Historians and archaeologists alike say that up to the time of the Great Zimbabwe Kingdom, a cow was most likely worth far more than any amount of gold. Even though gold was plentiful in the ground, many Africans at that time in history had no use for it.

Which brings us to the point.

Who decides what has value?

In an unthinking society, people just continue to assume that what their culture has at some point decided is of monetary value, just *is*. Without any further thought.

Many assume that the ancient people of central Africa just didn't know yet that gold was intrinsically valuable. That they merely hadn't been informed of this important fact. Nothing could be further from the truth. They simply had little use for gold as a substance at that time. Its inherent value or lack of value, wasn't something they needed to learn.

That doesn't change the fact, of course, that other cultures, both in Africa and elsewhere, had decided that gold was indeed highly valuable... to them. Nor that some of those cultures traversed Africa's jungles and savannahs, searching for the gold that lay across the continent in huge reserves, the largest gold reserves in the world. Some of the deepest mines in the world are in Africa.

The Gold Mines of Africa: highly, highly sought after.

Can you imagine what would happen if the wild herb growing rampant in your yard was suddenly worth millions of dollars? The herb that you have been stepping on trying to get to the car? Can you imagine what would happen as people descended in droves upon you, intent on having it at all costs? Setting up tents in the road and yard to harvest it and hurry off with it, with not even a thought that it belongs to you?

That is what happened in parts of Africa, with the gold.

For gold did have tremendous value to the people who came looking for it. They had use for it. Great prices were paid, and part of that price was in human lives. Great wealth came from the gold mines, both in the past and this very day. Parts of modern Africa, glittering parts, have been built on the money from gold.

Things actually aren't intrinsically valuable in terms of being worth millions of dollars, unless they are true necessities like food, water, clothing or shelter and are currently in short demand. Instead, people decide that things are valuable. They discover a valuable use for them, or, they just like them. Like million-dollar art or sculpture pieces.

What we value is, unfortunately, often arbitrary. It changes like the wind.

I heard of something on the stock market the other day that suddenly had magnificent value. It happened overnight; I had never heard of it until that day. That's not to say that it isn't of value. It may save lives. Or maybe it is actually useless or a whim.

Can you imagine a city where people decided that eradicating poverty or hunger from within their boundaries was the most valuable thing they could envision? So valuable they poured thousands upon thousands of dollars into it? Oh, I know, that would be a nice thing. But what if it wasn't just a nice thing? What if it was a passionate value? That it was talked about on every street corner of the town, over morning coffee in the restaurants? That people could hardly wait to arrive at work because they had thought of yet another idea to help the town? Because they viewed it not just as a wonderful, abstract, or self-righteous theory, charity, or a moral obligation, but as something to be proud of and to work hard for, because they thought it had *value*?

Value like gold.

Have you ever wondered what would happen if we would all just break out of the box we find ourselves in and make new decisions on what *we* think has value and what doesn't? Then simply act on those decisions?

In other words, what if our words and actions suddenly came into alignment?

There is nothing at all inherently wrong with gold, you know. It's a beautiful and quite useful substance of our earth.

Yet, Proverbs 16:16 says, *How much better to get wisdom than gold.*

That's because, when you have the wisdom, then you really know what to do with the gold.

Father, make my values line up with Yours. I thank You for the gold and all other things You have caused to be created on this earth. I thank You for the grains and the harvest. I thank You for it all. Please show us how to use these things, all of them, in ways that do not hurt others, but in ways that make sense to the best part of our nature, and to You.

51

Cardboard Homes

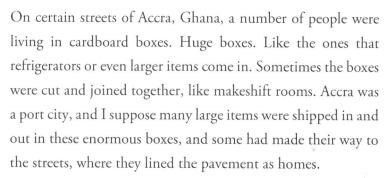

On certain streets of Accra, Ghana, a number of people were living in cardboard boxes. Huge boxes. Like the ones that refrigerators or even larger items come in. Sometimes the boxes were cut and joined together, like makeshift rooms. Accra was a port city, and I suppose many large items were shipped in and out in these enormous boxes, and some had made their way to the streets, where they lined the pavement as homes.

It was a tragedy to see. Little children wandering in and out of a box that had clearly been rained on—a sad shelter for a precious little life.

In the many years since I walked those streets, Ghana has worked hard to alleviate poverty and to bring down its rate of indigence though it certainly still exists.

Ghana is not alone, as far as countries trying to contain a growing poverty and hunger issue. Throughout much of Africa, as in the rest of the world, there is an ever-increasing divide between the rich and the poor, a growing chasm that must be narrowed or there will be excruciating repercussions around the globe.

As the debate continues on how to best fight poverty, whether through social responsibility, like programs and governments; or personal responsibility, such as the giving of our own resources, I continue to think that both seem helpful.

But, I do think that it's sometimes easy to look to programs and forget personal responsibility.

In the decrees of Moses, the yearlong tithe of the third and sixth years went to the poor. It seems a really good use of the tithe, and it makes me happy to know that God ordained it.

It has never computed well in my mind that some people are living in extraordinary wealth, while others, including children, are being evicted from the only roof over their heads, and thousands of children's arms are thinner than a wire, from starvation and malnourishment. It takes a frightening convolution of the mind to make this in any way okay.

It appears God does not find it acceptable either.

I have found a most interesting Scripture in the Bible.

One who is gracious to a poor man lends to the Lord, And He will repay him for his good deed (Proverbs 19:17 NASB).

Lends to God? Why does it say lend to God and not *gives* to God? In the original language, it indeed does say "lend." And it appears to be the only time such a phrase is used in terms of our giving.

It seems, to me at least, that this is of such utmost

importance to God that all gifts to the poor will indeed be repaid somehow—by God's decree, not because we may or may not *want* to be repaid, but because He considers helping the poor so important that it turns into a loan to Him.

God's original law also said that at harvest time people were never to go back and pick up all the many leftovers from the crops. All the grapes on the ground, all the grain, were left for those who needed it.

I believe that these original laws for behavior that God set down show us how He would have us think and act toward anyone in poverty, that He would have us offer them many ways to receive help.

The writer of the New Testament book of Hebrews tells us, *This is the covenant I will make with them after that time, says the Lord. I will put my laws in their hearts, and I will write them on their minds* (Hebrews 10:16).

How does it look to have the law regarding the poor written on our hearts? Making sure they have food? That their debts are forgiven and that we don't demand harsh payment of loans—that we don't lend with interest?

I think the way it looks is probably something life-changing. World-changing. I believe this was and is God's extraordinary blueprint on how to live and help people, and it's a brand new mindset.

I do know that when it rains, cardboard boxes are not a good protection from the elements and children get sick and things get ruined. Cardboard houses are not safe. I wouldn't want to ever live in one, and neither would you. No one would. No one should have to.

⎯⎯⎯✑⎯⎯⎯

Father, write Your beneficial law upon my heart. You have always had our good in mind; You have it in mind now. Let me shower that good upon everyone in need, from a heart filled with freedom and free from all grasping. And Father, if I or anyone I love is ever in poverty please help us and free us from it completely, and save us. Help us indeed to do unto others as we would want things done regarding us. In Jesus' name.

52

Race

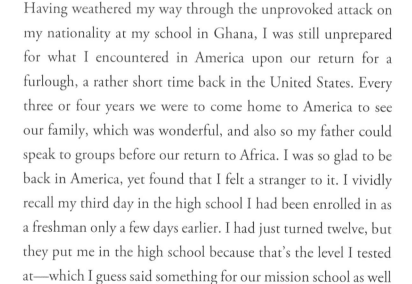

Having weathered my way through the unprovoked attack on my nationality at my school in Ghana, I was still unprepared for what I encountered in America upon our return for a furlough, a rather short time back in the United States. Every three or four years we were to come home to America to see our family, which was wonderful, and also so my father could speak to groups before our return to Africa. I was so glad to be back in America, yet found that I felt a stranger to it. I vividly recall my third day in the high school I had been enrolled in as a freshman only a few days earlier. I had just turned twelve, but they put me in the high school because that's the level I tested at—which I guess said something for our mission school as well as my school in Ghana. I would be at this high school for three months. I felt completely lost.

On that third day at high school, a large group of African American students were gathered on the wide steps between the first and second floor, most of them leaning over the step railings or over the second floor railings. A large group of white students were gathered in the expansive hallway below them, many of them lined up by the walls. The two groups were yelling at each other, with racist slurs and angry words being hurled loudly from one side to the other. I remember standing alone, looking back and forth between them, having no idea what I was to do or where I was to go. Not only did I not know anyone, I also did not know what new horror I was looking at. It had never occurred to me that America, my own country, was in such a state. I felt terrorized. I left; no one was noticing me anyway or seemed to particularly care that I was there. I went to the cafeteria and pulled out one of the brown trays on the rack, put food on it and sat down, alone. I wanted desperately to go home. Where had I ended up? This was unrecognizable to me. What sort of a place was this? Thoughts whirled through my mind, having nowhere to land.

One thing is for certain, race is surely not the only factor that people find to draw the lines of hatred over. A simple look at history proves this over and over. People of various races have often banded together, whether to form a cohesive political party or a side in a conflict, or for economic reasons, to hate some other group. And groups of the same race have often nearly eradicated each other, over strong differences, boundary lines, ethnicity, or the economics and nationalism of countries. Even a fleeting look at the history of Europe underscores this, with its various wars that laid waste to entire countries. And the wars of the Middle East. And the wars of Africa, long before the colonists ever arrived.

People seem easily capable of dividing themselves along any number of lines. The sooner we understand this, and stop making things just a racial problem, the sooner we will begin to find solutions. Because it's *not* just a racial problem. It's a very tragic problem of the human race. Hatred, and the subjugation and eradication of people for any reason, race or otherwise, is a disease.

But back to the subject of racial hatred, that despicable and vile form that human hatred can take. I learned an important lesson in Africa, in Zimbabwe, long ago. It was the words of my father. And he repeated it when we were back in America.

He looked me straight in the eye, as only he could, and said in a voice that carried so much presence, so much integrity.

"Never, ever put anyone down because of their race. Ever. Everyone is equal. Do you understand me?" I nodded and began to turn away.

But the look in his eye made me turn back.

"And never, ever, allow anyone to put you down because of your race. Ever. Everyone is equal. Do you understand me?"

I nodded again slowly.

I think of those words of his quite often. Very often, in fact. They have never left me. I have tried my best to live by them.

I wish I knew how to make the entire world live by them. I may be sadly simplistic, but those words seem to encapsulate the subject for me. Don't put anyone down. Don't let anyone put you down.

In other words, we've come right back to that same phrase that sounds truly simplistic in the face of the horrors humans have wrought on each other, but remains as true and profound as when Jesus first said it ...

Do to others as you would have them do to you (Luke 6:31).

———❧———

Father, I have no need to recount to You the tragedies people have wrought on one another from their hatreds, including their racial hatreds. You already know. You saw it. You see it. So I pray for help. I pray for an outpouring of Your Spirit that created us all and ask for Your help. No, plead for Your help. Please pour out upon us Your help, Your peace.

53

The Speaking of Words

The darker forms of certain religions were going on in Ghana, and in Zimbabwe, when we were there, just as they were in other places on earth. There were terrible rites being carried out in some places, animals being tortured for no reason, curses being put on people, and other such things.

I remember the day a young man back at our mission station was in a state of great panic, because a leading village man practicing the darker arts had cursed him and said that because he would not do as the local leader wanted, in three days he would see a snake cross his path, and he would fall down dead. This was terrorizing to our friend because this leader had made similar curses before regarding others, and they had come true. We prayed with our friend and claimed the protection of the name and power of Jesus.

The third day passed, no snake was seen on any path he walked, and the young man lived. God showed great power around us, many times over.

Whether it is someone practicing a dark form of religion, on any continent or whether it is a father or mother anywhere, calling their child by derogatory names… words matter. That parent, making dire pronouncements upon their poor child about their intelligence, looks or capabilities, is doing nothing more than practicing the old damaging art of "speaking words over people."

For that is much of what the dark arts are: an attempt at control by speaking words, with the addition of intense, laser-like focused thought and feeling. It doesn't matter how many rows of candles one lights, how many altars of any kind are erected, how many figurines, statues or totems are set up or bowed down to, how many potions are mixed and spoken over or how many psychological studies one cites as justification of what one is trying to imprint upon another person. Speaking negative or misleading words over people can be damaging.

There are people this day who are living under this damage, from their childhood or workplace, from cruel enemies or supposed friends… living under the effect of words said to them. And the people who spoke the hateful words are drunk on their victims' blood—on their life spirit.

The tongue has the power of life and death (Proverbs 18:21). Words carry power; it would be hard to overstate their importance. They can carry a positive, life-affirming power— containers that carry truth, authenticity and robust health into people's lives.

And they can carry darkness. A deceptive web of darkness that is hard to untangle.

We are responsible for our words, and for what we are really trying to gain in our use of them. It is vital that we never deceive ourselves regarding our speech, pretending to be doing good while having a heart that is jealous or of ill intent.

We are all familiar with those instances when we encounter someone who gives the appearance of saying something helpful or kind to us and yet we leave their presence feeling downcast and inexplicably harmed. Or the honey-filled words that encourage us to give up when we should not. In those cases, deception and darkness have penetrated whatever words are being used, *for the mouth speaks what the heart is full of* (Luke 6:45).

Our words, the nuances carried in them, and the thought-forms behind them, spring from the depths of our heart, from our motivations.

Often what people attribute to evil spirits is simply the work of human beings. And it's often the result of their words.

It does seem that evil entities and spirits can also get involved in the process. I think it's probably irrelevant to those evil spirits whether the individuals damaging others are jumping around in contortions, performing some solemn ritual, or if it is a lone, well-dressed woman in a high rise lacerating her young teenaged daughter with words that may imbed for a lifetime.

Evil is always after a life-damaging, life-limiting result.

It may be that if an evil spirit can also manage to get an animal or a person maimed and tortured in the process that it adds to their pleasure. I am no expert on them, but it seems likely. Darkness seems to enjoy vicarious suffering. But I think they couldn't care less about the trappings that we associate with the dark arts, the volumes of instructions, and the crafts and arts of the trade, as they are called. I doubt it. They know what and where the real damage is.

They know that when people speak words and use actions to manipulate, harm or to control others—to impose their personal will upon others—that the dark side is winning.

Yet, important as our words are, there is something that carries far more power than either our good words or our unhealthy words. A creative power above us all, whether we are human or other, dark or light.

And that is the Word of God.

The Word of the Ancient One rules.

Jesus, himself, when tempted in the desert by the devil, did not try to reason and come up with a lot of arguments or insist on a big encounter. He did not wave his arms and go into fits of yelling. Jesus did only one thing when faced with those awful words coming at him. He said, three times over, It is written… and then he recited the ancient Scriptures:

It is written… Man shall not live on bread alone, but on every word that comes from the mouth of God.

It is written… Do not put the Lord your God to the test.

It is written …Worship the Lord your God, and serve him

only.

The Bible says that after Jesus spoke those words the devil left. Just left. As it says in 2 Samuel 22:31: *The Lord's word is flawless; he shields all who take refuge in him.*

The plan of Jesus, I think, may be the best to use to protect ourselves from anyone making their bid for control.

——— ———

Lord, keep us from trying to control things. Help us instead to turn our lives over to You and to follow Your paths. Please put deep in our hearts the words Jesus said as he prayed for those following him... I have given them Your word... Sanctify them by the truth; Your word is truth. (John 17:14-17).

54

Life on the Coast

There is something wonderful about living near the ocean. The sea air is invigorating, yet somehow calming and the sound of the waves primal. The salt air adds a glow to the skin, and the water of the sea is exhilarating and healing. Oceans do not all look the same, just as coastlines don't. I'm sure oceanographers and marine biologists can see the differences in oceans quicker and far more accurately than I. They look different, they feel different.

We continued to live in our house in Ghana, the one that had been broken into and had flooded, for the rest of our time there.

Our guard also stayed on, doing a wonderful job every night. And we had taken over responsibility for a dog, who turned out to be something of a guard as well. He was a bush dog, and he got along well with both our guard and me. He had been handed down from a German doctor who was returning home and could not take the dog with him, first to the missionary family who had come to Ghana and laid the groundwork for the college, and now to us. He was a beautiful animal.

Sometimes in the late afternoons during those warm days near the ocean, after my piano lessons with my Polish teacher, and after my French tutoring, I would climb up on the red-tiled roof of our house for a bit, and sit there, high on the roof, just thinking about various things.

I don't know if he first saw me there or not, but it was not long before I was joined in the yard by a friend. A monkey was soon scampering into the yard, and I fed him each day, finding various little things to give him. I can still see his little arm reaching out to delicately take a peanut or a piece of banana from my open palm, making all his little noises. Such an intelligent and precious creature; a clever little thing too. I knew better than to attempt to domesticate him by taking him inside. A boy on our mission station back in Zimbabwe had tried just that with one of the monkeys that lived with us on our station. The monkey—though loving and fun—had managed to shred the curtains and do an astounding assortment of other major damage. They like to rummage through kitchens and bedrooms and can became territorial with certain family members. Monkeys aren't made to be bound up in a house like that. Because they are so oriented to familial or tribal thinking, they suffer tremendous psychological trauma when not allowed to live in their social units or are shifted from human to human, as pets. They take it personally.

Our wonderful Indian friends from the import store, of the Hindu faith, would invite us to their home where we were served magnificent Indian food. Sometimes the food was brought over from a well-known Indian restaurant in Accra that they had connections to. I remember having a freshly made, deeply rich and warm beverage served in a small, beautiful cup at their house, at a long low table over an exquisite Indian rug.

I was excited that in Accra there were, here and there, some black and white televisions. We did not have one, but some friends did, and some afternoons I would walk the mile to their home to see a television program about a mermaid, all done with marionettes. It had English subtitles, and I think was made in Denmark. There were only two programs on in the afternoon, and one station, but we felt very modern there in that house in front of the set. Quite different from the lack of outside communication I had grown accustomed to on the mission station.

To get to my Danish television program, during the afternoons in Accra, I had to cross a field that had anthills, and the anthills in Ghana are filled with stinging ants. Accra's name itself comes from the Akan language word for anthill.

I remember the one single night that we met with someone at the Pan American Hotel. I had never been there. The days had been so hot, and that night we sat on a long balcony by a cool fountain surrounded by greenery and beautiful lights on the path, and I had in front of me one single scoop of delicious, real ice cream, in a silver bowl on a little silver plate. I have never forgotten the beauty of that evening.

On Friday nights, my mother and I would sometimes attend the movie house in Accra. It was mostly older American movies—Westerns and such. The movie house had no roof, but was a square cement building of four walls, and folding chairs had been set up inside. When it rained, they just turned the movie off and shut down. It was there I saw my first movie about Alfred the Great and his battles with the Vikings, and I remained entranced with that time in history for a long time.

Everywhere in Accra, there were the seemingly omnipresent mammy wagons. I have heard that "mammy" comes from a Twi word, meaning a wealthy woman, but I don't know for sure. Mammy wagons were stalwart, open-sided bus-trucks that transported everything imaginable… adults, children, chickens, produce, goods to sell, belongings, whatever. There were so many of them. And many were in fact driven by women.

I felt so fortunate, after some months of being in Ghana, that my family was able to purchase one window air conditioner, which had just come on the market in Accra. It was put in my bedroom while my parents continued to suffer in the night heat. My parents, though, would come and sit under it some afternoons for ten minutes or so as they drank their coffee. It was boiling hot outside and in every other part of our house.

One July Fourth, The American Embassy had hot dogs, Coca-Cola, and other picnic food flown in from New York City. Every American citizen in Ghana received an invitation to come. There were not many Americans in Ghana at that time, but I do think most came. My friend from school, the young boy who had stood up for me, was there, as his family was associated with the Embassy staff. It had taken a lot of planning and effort for them to pull off their project of having the food brought in for the celebration.

So many memories of Ghana.

I loved the ocean; it was the first time I had lived near the sea. And we were extremely near it. My father baptized people in the Atlantic Ocean.

The Bible says that for everything there is a time, a season.

There is a time for everything, and a season for every activity under the heavens (Ecclesiastes 3:1).

I am glad that one of the seasons of my life has included living on the West African ocean and watching the golden sunsets.

Father, I pray that we can each embrace the seasons of our lives. And I pray that those seasons will be happy, and good ones, and that we will also stand with those who are in difficult seasons. But we pray for the good ones, for all of us.

55

The Prime Meridian

I stood on the coast of Ghana with my father, and he leaned over, one arm on my shoulder, and pointed out to sea with his other, past the riptides that coast is famous for, past the last rock we could see. It's a somewhat well-known rock, for straight beyond it, in the ocean, is what has sometimes been called the "center of the world."

We were standing on the Prime Meridian. It ran beneath our feet, and continued straight on, over the rock directly in front of us, with the waves breaking around it.

But, even more important, straight beyond where we were and beyond the rock, far out in the ocean's water, is the place where the Prime Meridian intersects the Equator.

The center of the world, in the terms we use for navigation and map-making, at least—0 longitude, and 0 latitude.

This is the point where they intersect.

It's easy to think that wherever we are, and wherever our

own people are from, is, more or less, the center of the world. It feels that way. It feels to us that what happens where we are has big consequences.

And it does. What happens where we live, wherever that currently happens to be, does matter. But where is the center of the world? There are so many theories about this subject. Is it the intriguing intersection of the Equator and the Prime Meridian?

Or is that the wrong question. Perhaps, more than *where* is the center of the world, the question should be, *who* is the center of the world.

I believe that our Creator is the center of this world and of the universe—that it is the creative force and power of the One who made it that holds the very atoms in place.

It's at the moment of acceptance—that the Creator is the center, the pivotal factor—that all falls into place, like one of those old children's puzzles when the large wooden pieces finally come together, clicking into place. If we are the center, we don't seem to know what we are doing. It may be a momentary, heady feeling to think that we are in that central position, but it quickly grows futile. If the Creator is the center, the One who knows what this is all about, then there is hope.

Our Creator is our plumb line. In the end, that is who the world belongs to. And, according to the Bible, we as humans were entrusted with it—to be caretakers. *Caretakers*, not rabid masters.

I loved standing there with my father on Ghana's coast,

looking out to the flowing, blue sea, with the western sun shining down upon it and the white caps foaming as they hit the huge rocks and the sand. Seeing that final rock, the last piece of land, before the spot, out there someplace, that could be the center of the world. Where east meets west and north meets south.

Where our own center is matters. If our center is God, we are headed to better times.

And I believe this for Ghana. It is my strong belief that the nation of Ghana, if it turns itself completely over to the one true God, has the chance to become one of the great nations of the earth. That they have what it takes. There is something powerful, something lively, something of valor in the people of Ghana.

As the powerful Omanhene of southeastern Ghana said on that long ago day when he graciously invited our college's teachers to his huge gathering: *Righteousness exalts a nation, but sin condemns any people.* His words, not mine. God's words.

I believe that Ghana has a chance to do something great. To become a place known for integrity, for a powerful work ethic, and a place that moves strongly to alleviate poverty and to make its citizens proud.

I hope it happens. I believe in them.

———

God, I pray that You would bless Ghana. That Your Spirit of truth and grace would come over that land, that Ghana would be known, far and wide, as a place where honesty is paramount, where business is done in a way that honors You. Where Your Word is followed. A place where the government and all such institutions put the people before their own interest. In other words, a place of real leadership. I pray for all Your people throughout Ghana.

56

Going Back

———— ⌘ ————

My parents decided, when I was a teenager, that I should live in America to attend high school and have braces put on my teeth. I lived with my brother Ron and his family. My brother Jim and his wife also lived nearby, so I was now situated with half of my family once again, this time on the other side of the ocean.

It was a massive adjustment for me, as the last full year of American school I had attended was second grade. My parents had returned to Ghana, and then—while I was still in America with my braces—they were asked to come back to Zimbabwe so my father could participate in the further establishment of the college there.

So early one summer, I, too, was flown back to Zimbabwe one last time, to reunite with my parents. The crisis that would eventually overtake Zimbabwe was moving under the surface, day by day, simmering like the bubbles rising from a long cooking soup. A missionary from New Zealand who had been in Zimbabwe for years ran a second time for government office and raised a loud voice on behalf of redistribution of land and for human rights. He was put under house arrest by the white Rhodesian government. An immigrant from Scotland, who had been mayor of a city, also spoke out for African rights. Their voices did not prevail.

I was given a formal letter from the governments of both America and Rhodesia to carry on my person at all times, allowing me to pass, in case I was questioned in my travel. It scared me, at times, to be wandering around the world with my important entrance papers to the land where my parents were, a land now under growing duress.

The college had finally moved from its many years on the mission station to what was then called Fort Victoria, now Masvingo, so that is where my parents were living. Fort Victoria was the oldest colonial settlement in Zimbabwe and was indeed originally built as a fort to protect against the first uprisings of the indigenous people against colonial rule.

Our old driver from the mission station was working on a road crew near Fort Victoria by then, and when he heard I had come back, he walked a number of miles just to see me and greet me. We had a nice evening with him. It was good to see him once again sitting at our kitchen table. The sister of one of the African women my mother knew from the mission station was also there, living in the township, and she, too was often at our kitchen table having tea with my mother.

The missionaries in Fort Victoria had started a church both in the white town and in the African township. They not only helped start the township church, they began holding highly sought after classes there during the week, training people so they could find meaningful employment. I recall seeing the lines of sewing machines, bought with mission money, on long, wooden tables and the women of the township learning to use them. These classes were an important effort that was a well-regarded endeavor on their part.

There were so many wonderful people living in the African township, and there were wonderful European families living in the white town.

Sometimes in life, as was the case with many of the missionaries in Fort Victoria back then, we find ourselves in a political or governmental system that we inherently disagree with but do not have the numbers yet to peacefully combat or change. At that point, as many people around the world are having to do at this very moment, what is left is to take all the steps we can think of to work toward and encourage the progress of what we know is right.

From Fort Victoria, our college moved to Salisbury, now Harare, as the mission was able to buy an old British hotel that had been vacated. So there we were, a bit lost among the remains of what had once been a remarkably swank estate, now somewhat run-down in places, but with a magnificent kitchen and staff, and huge fireplaces and large grounds. It was a sprawling, one level, white stone affair, with green grass and numerous gardens, the entire thing in various states of repair and disrepair. Some of the kitchen staff stayed on to work for the school, which was good, as the food was wonderful. Slowly we turned the rooms into classrooms, and the hotel became a college.

It was a magnificent summer in some ways and not in others. I got to experience life in a town and city in Rhodesia, even if only briefly—something so different from my years in the bush. I got to live in a city neighborhood in Zimbabwe, even for just months, and walk downtown to the main street with its wide and beautiful, jacaranda-lined road. I was also able to see firsthand how the African people in the townships, also known as locations, were having to deal with the hardship of being an underclass, without rights in countless ways. It was wrong, so very wrong, and no words or theories could make it right. Things simply needed to change.

We took one trip, that always long trip, back out to the mission station. Even by that summer it had changed. It was more built up, and there were small signs of more modern civilization here and there. Better for them, and I was glad, but a loss to me to know I could never see it again the way it once was. Only a handful of people would now remember it the way it once had been.

Even now, just the names of each of those remote mission stations out in the bush country, where our missionaries lived—those names still bring a pang of wistfulness to me, and a smile of happiness to my face.

The unrest that would devastate Zimbabwe was growing. By the time the war was over, the old mission station would be partially overrun. The mission doctor who had originally overseen the building of the hospital had returned to try to save it and was the last of the missionaries to leave the station. He had a serious altercation with a young Rhodesian officer over the beating of one of our most beloved African teachers. Confusion ensued and he was informed that he had been targeted. He was told that an elite military unit had targeted him and was coming for him as he was considered to be a person harboring terrorists. Later there was information that actually quite the opposite had been true and that the terrorists were the ones attempting to find and kill him because they thought he must be siding with the government. It was a highly charged and dangerous situation. At one point rebel soldiers came inside the halls of the hospital and gunfire was heard.

The doctor waited until nightfall then he climbed the kopje at the far end of our station, the one behind the house we had lived in, and made his way through the bush in the dark to his small plane sitting on the mission landing strip. He took off in the darkness, flying as low to the ground as possible all the way to the relative safety of Chiredzi.

So many people were killed across the country, so much horrifying destruction wrought. It was distressing beyond measure to read the letters that we received from African friends for many years, the news that made its way out, of the chaos and pain. We knew these people. We loved them. The magnificent people of Zimbabwe.

Volumes have been written about the Rhodesian Bush War. Highly trained guerilla fighters came across the north and east borders. Many tribesmen who refused to harbor them were brutally hacked to death with machetes and the young men kidnapped. Other tribesmen gladly welcomed them. The white community splintered in places due to conflicting ideas regarding the situation. Among others in that European community, there was a unified approach.

A greatly respected and loved Chief on the Matsai Reserve was murdered by the guerillas. They also killed one of the African preachers from another of our remote mission stations. Many Africans in the bush country were atrociously tortured and butchered to death, their cattle also tortured and slaughtered. A number of European ranchers and farmers, along with their families, were ruthlessly massacred.

There were not just two sides in the conflict, clearly drawn. So many people had competing loyalties, ideas at odds with one another on how to stop the violence or even how to think about it.

In the end, as is true in most wars, people of all persuasions finally hunkered down to try to save their own homes, crops, livestock, and, above all else, their children.

War is deadly, and I am no expert on it.

I have come to the place in life where I believe that wherever we live it is of vital importance to do all we can to ensure that everyone is treated with integrity, justice, fairness and equality on all counts. I don't see anything else working anywhere. And sometimes even that is not enough to hold the peace.

One of the original mission station nurses bravely went back alone, just after the war, when things were very dangerous, to bring the hospital back and restart the nursing assistant program. Upon her return to the mission station, she found that the Zimbabweans, under duress, had done a remarkable job of keeping at least the critical parts of the hospital operational. She then set about, with the aid of a remarkable Zimbabwean woman still there, to put the nursing training program back on its feet so they could continue to operate it as well.

Surely, one of the most naturally beautiful places on earth had entered the crucible. A trial by fire. It has not completely come out of that crucible. The blood, both past and present, now spilt on the soil of Zimbabwe is overwhelming. It is heartbreaking beyond all words.

There is a famous song in Zimbabwe, sung by many, that says it well… God bless Africa. *Ishe Komborera Africa.*

And words from another one, the new national anthem, "And may the Almighty protect and bless our land."

God, put this nation, this important nation of Zimbabwe, finally, truly, back on its feet. Bring freedom, wholeness, health, safety, and truth into the public sphere and pour out Your Spirit upon the beautiful people of Zimbabwe. Grant them real peace. Give them a future that is filled with blessing. Please do a miracle and ease the burden of great sorrow that has been visited upon them.

57

Angels Unawares

When I was fourteen years old, at the end of that summer in Zimbabwe, I was sent back to America alone. In those days, it was a very different trip than it is now. Even close to his dying day, my father remained unsure how he could have made the decision to send me back alone, without someone to accompany me, even though he had carefully tried to arrange the flight details for my safety. The person who had been scheduled to travel with me had plans altered at the last minute, and there was no transferable ticket. Flights in those days were extremely expensive, but I needed to go as my school in America was about to start, and there was no extra money now for another person to fly with me. Children, even teenagers, seldom made transatlantic flights alone in those days, but the life of missionaries seems fraught with adventure, if anything.

Traveling long before the advent of cell phones, computers, and the like, I became adrift in the wide world, out of communication with every person I knew.

My plane landed in Angola, in the middle of the night, and everyone but me disembarked while men in white garments came in, each carrying one of the old pump spray canisters with the pump held out to the side. The captain had warned the passengers that the plane was going to be completely fumigated before takeoff and passengers who were concerned for health reasons should disembark.

I looked out the plane window to the little airport in the distance, cupping my hands on the window to try to see it across the tarmac. It looked to be a long, dark walk across the tarmac to the small airport. I had not liked the look of two of the European men on the plane with me, they seemed unsavory characters, and they kept eyeing me strangely. I did not like the idea of walking alone across that dark area.

I was the only passenger who stayed aboard. The mist from the fumigant was terrible. I have never heard what might have been going on in Angola at the time, to engender this activity. Our plane flew on to Geneva and then finally I was on a flight to Heathrow in London.

Be not forgetful to entertain strangers: for thereby some have entertained angels unawares (Hebrews 13:2 KJV).

On that flight, I couldn't help but notice the incredible stewardess who made her way up and down the aisle with the others. Among the beautiful girls, she was astounding, and not just because of her natural good looks. She was literally covered in sharply defined makeup. I was mesmerized by the blue eye shadow that ran from her eye clear up to her brow. Bright and powerful, it was all I could see.

I was coming from a place where no one, at least that I knew of, wore much in the way of make up at all, and even the girls in boarding schools in the cities were mostly fresh-faced and scrubbed in their uniforms. I couldn't take my eyes off of the stewardess. Each time that she walked by my seat, with her poise and self-sufficiency, I was glued to the sight of the brilliant smudges of bright blue. Paint. That's all I could think of. Those painted eyes overshadowed the boldly drawn brows and the striking red defined lips.

I disembarked in London and found my way to the airline desk to be met with unanticipated and most disturbing news. The British government had just put a ban on all passengers disembarking any plane from Rhodesia. Why they couldn't get this figured out before our planes landed that day I've never learned. The airlines had told my father there would be no layovers for me, only brief stops. But the businesslike man behind the desk told me in no uncertain terms that I would not be able to leave England for three days. We had to be cleared.

Some years earlier, when I had still been living on the mission station, the white government of Rhodesia had declared independence from Britain's Commonwealth, and Britain had refused to recognize the new government because they would not allow African majority rule. But that had been some time back, and although tensions were high, this turn of events at the airport was unexpected. I stood there, on my side of his desk, a lone girl, holding the little blue satchel that I had carried with me around the world.

Finally, I went and sat down on a bench, with my satchel on my lap, and stared at the wall. There was no hope of reaching my parents or anyone else, either on the mission station or in the town, wherever they might be. The first transatlantic phone cable had been laid under the ocean only a year after I was born so long distance calls were still not a particularly commonplace thing. The station, of course, didn't even have outside phones, and phone calls in general had involved us scheduling a time to make the journey to a city, scheduling the overseas call a month in advance, and maybe finally hearing the static intermingled with a voice on the other end. But even in the city where my parents most likely were, there was simply no way to get through so quickly.

I tried to place a complicated long distance call to one of my brothers in America from a large public pay phone on the wall—but to no avail. I realized then that they wouldn't even know what had happened to me. At last, I went back to my bench and sat. I tried to formulate a plan to find some sort of hotel for my days alone in London—my father had made sure I had traveler's checks as he knew I would be entirely on my own and out of communication with everyone—then I could set about trying to find a way to send someone a telegram from there.

I sat on for quite some time, in the same spot, deeply not

wanting to leave the supposed safety of the airport.

Suddenly, I heard a voice behind me, clearly speaking to me, yet I knew absolutely no one. I was alone.

"Why are you still here? Weren't you going on to America?"

I turned to face the blue-shadowed wonder. Her hair was an amazing blonde concoction such as I had never seen in all my life. Her perfume was powerful and beautiful.

I told her my story and pointed to the airline desk, explaining how none of the passengers from Rhodesia could leave. She stood staring at me, aghast. Furious. Her eyes were flashing, causing me to stare even further in silent shock and bewilderment at the blueness. She rose to her full stature, which was very tall—and marched off. I watched her go. A Valkyrie. A Warrior Princess. A being from another world.

I watched in awe and almost fear as she strode over like a Germanic princess to the desk. I could hear only phrases floating back to me... "a child." "Whatever are you thinking?" "Alone in London." "Get her on a plane now, I tell you. Now." "Ridiculous." "I'll see to it myself." I could only catch part of the words, the accent was so strong. The man behind the desk seemed nearly as cowed by her as I was. She took no back talk. She brooked no opposition.

Within the hour, papers had been signed and stamped, waivers given, and I was on my way to the city of Chicago. I boarded the plane, satchel in hand and sat down, staring ahead. My stewardess was not on this flight. I never saw her again.

The angel of the Lord encamps around those who fear him, and he delivers them (Psalm 34:7).

To this day, whenever I see an overly made up woman, no matter how garish, I smile. Sometimes I feel a small tear form in my eye. She makes me think of one of the most wonderful memories of my life. When a perfect stranger stood up for me in one of the most powerful ways I had ever seen.

Angels unawares. You never do really know.

I do know that I'm so grateful for the blue-shadowed, blue-eyed wonder woman.

Father, let me be an instrument of Your help. Don't allow me to overlook the need of the smallest and most insignificant of Your creation. They may need my help the most, the ones who stand where no one else but me is looking. And also, Lord, always send Your help to me, too, whether an unrecognizable angel or a person, when no one else is noticing my dilemma. In Jesus' Name. Amen.

58

The First Missionaries

Did we go to Africa or did Africa come to us?

The first time I heard such a question I was baffled. But a stronger student of history would have had no trouble with it. They would have known that some of the oldest churches in the world were in Africa. That some of the first missionaries came from Africa.

Long before the Western World ever heard the gospel, Africa believed.

I am dismayed when I hear people talk of how Europeans or Americans took the gospel to Africa, without any mention of the many, from various places, who brought the gospel to their own peoples.

My people, too; my ancestors, came from the lands of the Gentiles. So many of us, from the lands where people had to come and bring us news of the Messiah, would do well to be grateful, I think, instead of proud. We were the lands and the peoples who were once in darkness.

Gentile... A Latin word used for the original Hebrew word in the Scriptures that meant *the peoples*. And in Greek, "the ethnicities." The nations—those lands of all the peoples, where the light for revelation to the nations was brought.

Yes, missionaries from the West did go to Africa, some at great risk. But the Africans also came, at great risk.

No European country knew the good news of Jesus until missionaries—believers—from the Middle East and Africa showed up on their doorstep. Many of the early church fathers were Africans.

In Gaza, a disciple named Philip baptized an Ethiopian in 34 A.D., a man who was already a student of the Scriptures— he was reading the book of Isaiah when Philip met up with him. The Ethiopian, who was the Finance Minister in charge of the Queen of Ethiopia's treasury, was on the road leaving Jerusalem, making his way back to Ethiopia, most likely to the Kingdom of Meroe.

The apostle Philip made his way to Carthage in Tunisia to spread the news of Jesus. Some historians believe that the apostle Mark was in Egypt by 42 A.D. In Acts 11:20, we read that a believer from Cyrene in North Africa, in ancient Libya, came and preached the gospel to the Greeks in Antioch. Churches had been planted in Algeria by the year 100 A.D. In 197 A.D. the author Tertullian wrote that Christianity had permeated all ranks of society through North Africa.

Now some of those oldest churches lay in ruins.

Will this fate be what happens to America and the Western World? Will our churches lay in ruins, forgotten? Oh, I deeply hope not.

But Africa also gives us hope. For even if those oldest churches lay in ruins, many new ones are being started and rising up all across the continent.

The fact is that over the course of history, the missionaries have come from everywhere and have gone everywhere. To the West, to the East. To the North and the South. I don't know who was first, it depends on just how far back one wants to go. But they need to still come. They need to still go. Because huge parts of the world that once knew seem to know no longer.

There are now many churches in Africa. Some are the legacy of missionaries, many are indigenous churches, African-initiated churches. As is true for me and my own ancestors, none of us can fully trace the steps back to where those who went before us first heard the gospel, and from whom. But the point that matters is that we did hear it.

The word we now use—missionary—is not in any of the oldest texts of the Bible. It is not a word that was directly translated from any of the original languages the Bible was written in. Instead, the word derives from a Latin word, and first came into prominent use by the Jesuits in the Middle Ages. But the concept, "those who are sent out" is certainly throughout the Bible.

Today, churches in Africa are sending missionaries around the world, including to the United States and Europe, which is an extremely meaningful thing, but in doing so they are sending their missionaries into what has become one of the most hazardous and difficult of current missionary fields.

The current cultures of this world are pervasive entities; it takes a strong will and the empowering of God to not fall prey to the spirits of the age.

America, my country that I so care about, and that has so many fine people in it who do so much good, has, as many countries before it, allowed perversions and degradation to spill out from it. But this time, unlike those older nations before it, those degradations are spilling out across vast airwaves, through international satellite feeds, across a worldwide Internet, like a polluted, filthy waterfall. America is most certainly not alone in this, in today's world. And all of us, everywhere, need the help of the African missionaries, of any missionaries, from anywhere, who can stand for truth.

But mostly, we need great prayer.

The African Christians that we worked alongside in Ghana once told my family, "You loved us too much." The statement, said with heartfelt sincerity, still brings tears to my eyes. I would ask them, and all places where the church is now rising powerfully, I would cry out, "Please pray for my country, too, please love us now with the truth, *the truth of the gospel*, before we go down."

But—we have our great prophetic word, we still have the great hope for all of us. That Jesus is the light for revelation to the Gentiles. And that word will not go away. I cling to that phrase, that prophecy said over the Messiah, by Simeon, in the temple so long ago as he held the young Jesus in his arms: *For my eyes have seen your salvation, which you have prepared in the sight of all nations: a light for revelation to the Gentiles...* (Luke 2:30-32).

And that Messiah Yeshua—translated to the English as Jesus—said, *Go into all the world and preach the gospel to all creation* (Mark 16:15). It's a tall order, but He said it, so it can be done.

It gives one pause to think.

Could it happen?

Could it be that it is in our generations that the whole world *could* know the gospel at once? At the same time?

Could we do it, with God's help?

Help us not to think small, Lord. To not think in terms of the world's limitations. Could we? Could we reach the entire world in our current generation? Give us a new and fresh vision. Embolden us. Let us not be hampered by small thinking. Let us go forward with joy, laughter, resources, boldness, and the power of the Holy Spirit. Break us out of our boxes, Lord. Show us Your vision for our generations.

59

Blood of the Martyrs

I was only eight years old when I first heard of martyrs. I was sitting in the chapel service that was held each day at Johnson Bible College, back in Tennessee. The tragic news that three women associated with the school had been shot down and then knifed to death in the Congo had just been announced. They were victims of the beginning unrest that would, many years later, envelope the entire Congo. A gasp went up from the crowd, and then a deafening silence fell, interrupted only by crying from various quarters of the building from friends who knew them. At eight, I could only piece together that they had been ruthlessly killed, that the details were too vivid to announce except in private, and that it had to do with their faith, and being very much in the wrong place at the wrong time.

It had not been long before that, that my father first went to Africa. Aside from the pictures that he brought back, one thought in the back of my mind was the memory of the three murdered women. So, it was vaguely unsettling news to me to hear we were soon to be on our own way to Africa.

We certainly did not suffer martyrdom in Africa. Far from it. But other missionaries before and after us did. And most certainly many African people have. Africa has seen many martyrs for the Christian faith.

In the second century, even though the Roman Emperor Septimius Severus was himself born in Africa, violent persecution against Christians in Africa broke out. An individual accused of being a Christian was given the choice of either cursing the name of their Savior and making an offering to the Roman gods or facing execution. As was true elsewhere in that Empire, under various Roman Emperors, numerous African Christians were persecuted and killed for their faith, refusing to renounce their beliefs. Many were burned at the stake. Numbers of them were killed for refusing to submit their Scriptures to be burned.

Many historians think the persecution of African Christians was intense even under the famed Marcus Aurelius. Geiseric of the Vandals brought 80,000 people into Africa to lay siege to it around 430 A.D. Many Christians were martyred, and the famous Augustine, also born in Africa, died while the battles raged as he struggled from his deathbed to save the library at Hippo.

As history has marched on, thousands of African Christians have lost their lives, in Sudan, Uganda, the Congo and in many other places for refusing to renounce their faith. Or simply for being *of* the Christian faith. Slaughtered before they even had the chance to speak. Thousands more have suffered long years of agony and persecution, including being kidnapped, imprisoned, or sold as part of the current, modern day slave trade.

Africa is not alone in its history of Christian martyrs. It was the author of the book of Hebrews who wrote of those great saints of old... *Some faced jeers and flogging, and even chains and imprisonment. They were put to death by stoning; they were sawed in two; they were killed by the sword... persecuted and mistreated—the world was not worthy of them* (Hebrews 11:36-38). But the writer of Hebrews also said of those ancient saints: *who through faith... shut the mouths of lions, quenched the fury of the flames, and escaped the edge of the sword; whose weakness was turned to strength; and who became powerful... women received back their dead, raised to life again* (Hebrews 11:32-34).

I don't know why some face the sword for their faith and others are brought to major victories over the evil in front of them. And sometimes it is the same people who experience both. I do know that we need to be prepared for both. We will probably not know until it is upon us if we have been called to follow Jesus to our earthly demise, or if we will be the instruments of powerful miracles of deliverance. I think Esther had it right when she said, of her decision to try to save her people, *And if I perish, I perish* (Esther 4:16). Because she truly did not know which way it would go, or how it would all turn out; she only knew what she had to do.

And that is how it was for us. We went to Africa, half a century ago because we felt it was what God really wanted us to do. And in the end, it was one of the greatest gifts of my life. But we went because we felt led to, not because we knew ahead of time how it would go.

It is a tragedy of human history, past and present, that there are individuals among us who will kill a person because they believe differently. I consider myself fortunate to have friends from every major religion, and also from other lesser known belief systems, and they are all generous, peace-loving people and not one would consider murder because someone believed differently. To a person, each of them wants to live in a world where communication and peace flourishes. But there are clearly people who think different—terribly different.

I don't know why the three girls in the Congo died so horribly, so long ago. But I do believe that their work and their lives matter just as much in the final story as those of us who have continued living on the earth. And I am telling a fragment, a memory, of their story now, so long removed. I wish I could tell you their names, but my eight-year-old mind didn't retain that piece of information that day, only the horror of the events.

But God does know their names. He knows the names of all the martyrs, in Africa and elsewhere.

In the book of Revelation, there is a famous scripture of the martyrs, now with God, calling out to ask when those who caused their martyrdom will be judged.

When he opened the fifth seal, I saw under the altar the souls of those who had been slain because of the word of God and the testimony they had maintained. They called out in a loud voice, "How long, Sovereign Lord, holy and true, until you judge the inhabitants of the earth and avenge our blood?" (Revelation 6:9-10).

They are close to God, even now, it seems.

Waiting.

Waiting, for something He is going to do.

I find that an extremely sobering thought.

Father I pray that no one I know will be called on to die for their faith. But I also pray that they, and I, will have the courage to do so should it ever be required of us. There are things in life that we cannot understand on this side of the veil, on this side of the future. The terrible fact that there are people on this earth who would kill because someone believes differently than they do is one of those things. But we see it. We see it around us. Give us courage to face whatever befalls us. But also give us protection. In the name of Jesus.

60

Time Moves On

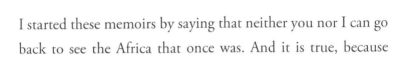

I started these memoirs by saying that neither you nor I can go back to see the Africa that once was. And it is true, because time moves on.

Just as in all other places and cultures, including my own, we can only catch glimpses of the past. I never knew the Africa that existed years before I arrived, but I caught the astounding fading glimpses of it. Amazing glimpses. And those going now will never see the Africa that I saw, in its last moments before we entered this highly connected, technological and commercial age.

Now we find ourselves taking pictures of the Africa of today on our cell phones and digital cameras and sending them instantaneously around the world. This very day I sat at my desk and emailed and exchanged social media with a friend in Cape Town. Recently, I heard a man from Togo say that 85 percent of the population in his nation, including those in rural areas, have cell phones. That changes everything. Places are no longer in such isolation.

But… time is supposed to move on. It may continue in one direction or take a completely unexpected turn, but it was created to move forward. As interesting, and, perhaps even enlightening, as it may be to look back to the very different past, we were not meant to stay there. We are meant to live today, engage what is current and make our lives count in the present. It's where our power is. It's where our lives are.

Our mission station, Mashoko Mission, still stands today, as a Christian medical area with schools and many surrounding churches. Although not nearly as remote, it has doubled in size, and is equipped with computers, outside communication, and even has a store… Still in the bush country, but more modern. It currently performs more than 2,000 surgical operations each year, has approximately 60,000 patients per year and an average of 200 babies are delivered there each month. There is a dental unit, as well as home-based AIDS care. In addition, the hospital has given rise to four other hospitals and clinics in various places. Thousands of people survived droughts in recent years because of the mission itself. The original hospital has in the ensuing years trained more than one thousand nurses. Also, most of the many surrounding churches were founded by individuals who first heard the gospel at the mission. It is an amazing legacy to those who served God and the people of Zimbabwe the best they knew how over half a century ago, and before. And it currently is and will be an outstanding legacy to the Zimbabweans who now run it, which is what we always wanted. It was the goal all along. Unquestionably the goal.

The roads are still not perfect getting out there, they say, but far better than long ago, and bridges have been built... though I hear that the Turgwe still floods across those bridges at times.

All across Zimbabwe the church is strong. The Chiredzi and Hippo Valley missions—where we would drive in our old dusty Peugeot—are also still growing and have risen to the challenge of the AIDS crisis that is ravaging the land. The original Bible College that moved to the city, stayed. The many individuals who were trained in the Bible College are in various places now, doing outstanding work.

I know for a fact that I have never met a people of such general kindness and organic dignity as the indigenous people of Zimbabwe. Their broad smiles and laughter and warmth stay with me to this day.

The college in Ghana where my father was the president is now one of the largest Christian Universities in Africa. It brings a tear to my eye to remember the little building we started in, the little band of missionaries and Ghanaians posing for a picture in front of that building.

I have heard so many individuals from so many ethnicities say that when they go to Africa they have the unusual feeling of going back to something, of getting in touch with something forgotten. From a woman of Scottish descent to a woman from

Australia, people say that when they set foot in Africa they feel like they have simply come home. Why is it that so very many of us from a range of countries feel a strange, drawing connection to this one continent—a place which must hold fragments of the ancestry of many, many people.

Africa calls out. But many of her children never come home. The Diaspora and pillaging of Africa have been profound.

On my last trip home from Africa, I flew over vast Kilimanjaro, looking down at the snowy volcano top, and as we passed, I drifted off to sleep in the airplane seat. Perhaps Africa has been in my dreams ever since. Perhaps it will never leave.

Other people who have gone to Africa, or for whom Africa is their homeland, may have very different experiences than I did. They may see things differently. But these are my experiences, and this is what happened to me, and what I learned.

If my stories have had any effect on you, if they have mattered, then I hope it is in this… that you will pray for Africa. That you will at least say one prayer. For a truly free Africa, a hope-filled Africa, a healthy Africa, a peaceful and prosperous Africa, a believing Africa. Pray that the sun always rises gloriously over the continent of Africa.

An African Sun.

As it should be.

AFTERWORD

Did you enjoy this book? Have you found it meaningful? If so, please consider leaving a review on Goodreads or your favorite book-related site. Thank you.

ABOUT THE AUTHOR

Mary Ann Simkins spent her childhood in Ghana, Zimbabwe and the United States. So far she has traveled to twenty-two countries and found every single one of them to be interesting and intriguing.

Mary Ann is very committed to aiding organizations around the world that are feeding and caring for women and children, for those rescuing and protecting animals in need, and to those working to protect and care for the environment of our God-given, gorgeous blue planet.

CONNECT WITH MARY ANN SIMKINS

To learn more about Mary Ann Simkins and her writing, visit her online!
Website: maryannsimkins.com
Facebook: facebook.com/authormaryannsimkins
Twitter: twitter.com/maryannsimkins

Made in the
USA
Monee, IL